Maltese

AMY FERNANDEZ

Maltese

Project Team
Editor: Heather Russell-Revesz
Copy Editor: Stephanie Fornino
Interior Design: Leah Lococo Ltd. and Stephanie Krautheim
Design Layout: Angela Stanford

T.F.H. Publications
President/CEO: Glen S. Axelrod
Executive Vice President: Mark E. Johnson
Publisher: Christopher T. Reggio
Production Manager: Kathy Bontz

T.F.H. Publications, Inc.
One TFH Plaza
Third and Union Avenues
Neptune City, NJ 07753

Discovery Communications, Inc.
  Book Development Team
Marjorie Kaplan, President, Animal Planet Media
Carol LeBlanc, Vice President, Licensing
Elizabeth Bakacs, Vice President, Creative Services
Brigid Ferraro, Director, Licensing
Peggy Ang, Director, Animal Planet Marketing
Caitlin Erb, Licensing Specialist

Printed and bound in China.
09 10 11 12 13   5 7 9 8 6 4

ISBN 978-0-7938-3772-4

Library of Congress Cataloging-in-Publication Data
Fernandez, Amy.
  Maltese / Amy Fernandez.
     p. cm. – (Animal Planet pet care library)
  Includes index.
  ISBN-13: 978-0-7938-3772-4 (alk. paper) 1. Maltese dog I. Title.
  SF429.M25F37 2007
  636.76–dc22
  2006031823

The Leader in Responsible Animal Care for Over 50 Years!®

www.tfh.com

Table of Contents

Chapter 1

Why I Adore My

Maltese

They may not herd sheep or hunt wolves, but don't make the mistake of thinking that a Maltese is merely a pretty face and a fancy coat. These little white dogs fulfill a vital function, and they take their job as seriously as any other breed. The "comfort dog" has played a time-honored role in the history of the human/canine relationship. Their ability to comfort us during bad times and help us celebrate good times has contributed to human mental, if not physical, well-being since antiquity.

Although these benefits were recognized, obviously, humans had no way to scientifically document them until recently. Today, Maltese put these gifts to work as service dogs, therapy dogs, and cherished pets.

History of the Maltese

Many details of Maltese history remain puzzling. The name has been known since Greek and Roman times. However, it's questionable whether the ancient "Dog of Malta" bears much resemblance to the Maltese we are familiar with today. Many breed historians suspect this was a catchall phrase used to describe a variety of small dogs native to Mediterranean Malta or the Adriatic Island of Melita. There are a number of islands similarly named all along the northern Mediterranean, and for centuries, white lapdogs were bred and exported from the region. "Dogs of Malta" probably referred to varying types, which could have included forerunners of several modern breeds in addition to Maltese.

Strabo, the most quoted Roman on the subject of Maltese, had this to say in 60 BCE: "There is a town of Sicily called Melita, from whence are transported many fine little dogs called Meliei canes. They were accounted the jewels of women but now the town is possessed by fishermen and there is no such reckoning made of those tender little dogs, for they are not bigger than common ferrets or weasels. Yet they are not small in

White lapdogs were bred for centuries along the northern Mediterranean.

Famous Maltese Lovers

If the Maltese is your favorite breed, you are in good company. Some of the breed's well-known admirers include Queen Elizabeth I, Queen Victoria, Liberace, Tallulah Bankhead, Gary Cooper, and Elizabeth Taylor.

after receiving one as a gift from the Sultan of Turkey. Dr. Johannes Caius, canine historian and physician to Her Majesty, described the breed in 1576, in *English Dogges*, "They are called Meliti, on the Island of Malta. They are very small indeed and chiefly sought after for the pleasure and amusement of women who carried them in their arms, their bosoms, and their beds."

Maltese remained popular for centuries, although artistic renderings reveal that they varied substantially in shape, size, and coat. Perhaps the earliest evidence of the Maltese as we know him today is found in Sir Joshua Reynold's 1763 portrait of Nellie O'Brien, depicted holding a clearly recognizable modern-type Maltese. The famed animal artist Edwin Landseer portrayed the breed in 1830 and 1851. Both paintings also show clear similarities to modern day Maltese.

Maltese were among the first breeds exhibited at early dog shows in the 1860s and '70s, and grooming and presentation were no less

understanding nor mutable in their love to men: for which cause they are also nourished tenderly for pleasure: whereupon came the proverb 'Melitea Catella' for one nourished for pleasure, and 'Canis Digno Throno' because princes hold them in their hands sitting upon their estate."

The Maltese in England

By the Middle Ages, an extensive trade network linked Europe and the Mediterranean, making imported luxuries widely available. Little white Maltese dogs became the treasured pets of European royalty. England's Queen Elizabeth I set the pace in Maltese popularity

Maltese dogs were treasured pets of European royalty.

important back then. Nineteenth century dog show reports described methods used to whiten coats and protect them with braids, hair clips, snoods, and boots.

Mr. Robert Manville developed the most famous nineteenth century strain

SENIOR DOG TIP

When Is My Maltese a Senior?

Toy breeds are noted for a long lifespan, and longevity and relative good health represent major advantages of Maltese ownership. "I have to say that by and large, Maltese live to a good age. I would say 12 to 15 is about norm," says Maltese breeder Vicki Fierheller. Maltese may begin to slow down a bit after age eight or nine, but you can expect a well-bred, well-cared-for dog to give you many years of companionship. Fierheller notes, "I'm not really sure if there are specific old age disorders. They don't even seem to develop cataracts or deafness until they are very elderly. I've seen the occasional heart problem, but again, quite late in age. One thing about Maltese—they seem to be very healthy and playful until a ripe old age."

of Maltese during the 1860s, and the breed continued to enjoy widespread popularity until the hardships of World War I curtailed much dog breeding and dog showing in Europe.

After the war, efforts were made to reestablish the breed using stock imported from Malta. This resulted in great variations in size, because some of the imported dogs were said to have been nearly as large as sheepdogs. Eventually, some correctly sized dogs were located in Holland and Germany. These were incorporated into breeding programs to help revive the English Maltese stock.

The Maltese in America

As in England, Maltese made an appearance at the earliest American dog shows. The catalog for the first Westminster dog show in 1877 contains the entry for a Maltese "Lion Dog." A Maltese Skye Terrier was exhibited at Westminster two years later, in 1879. The first Maltese were entered in the American Kennel Club (AKC) studbook, Topsy and Snips, in 1888, just four years after the formation of the AKC.

In contrast to the breed's longstanding popularity in Europe and England, the Maltese remained rare in America. Writing in 1905, the preeminent American dog authority James Watson stated, "Such a thing as a good Maltese dog is all but unknown in this country, and few seem to care about taking up the fancy." Less than 1,500 Maltese were AKC registered between 1888 and 1950. The Maltese was perpetuated in America by a few dedicated breeders such as

Mrs. Harry Peaster's La Rex Doll kennel in Philadelphia and the famous Villa Malta kennel of Dr. Vincenzo Calvaresi.

During the 1950s, the Maltese began to attract more interest, and the Maltese Club of America was founded in 1961. By the 1970s, the breed achieved a level of popularity that continues today.

Appearance

Chances are, you were first attracted to the Maltese because of their charming appearance. You may have seen one at a dog show or walking down the street, or you may have viewed a picture in a dog book. Regardless of how or where you first became acquainted with the Maltese, you were probably captivated by the entire delightful package—complete with bows on top.

The recipe for this irresistible combination of tiny size, dazzling white coat, and adorable expression remains a mystery, but dog clubs do have a written "standard" that describes what an ideal Maltese should look like. This standard is used for judging dog shows and also gives breeders a "blueprint" for their breeding program.

Size

Ideally, a Maltese should weigh from 4 to 6 pounds (1.8 to 2.7 kg) and never

The Maltese has a long, flowing coat.

more than 7 pounds (3.2 kg). Although the Maltese is not the smallest toy breed, it is definitely a dainty, portable lapdog. However, beware of any breeder who advertises Maltese puppies as "miniature" or "teacup." These are not recognized varieties, and serious breeders would never use these descriptions.

Coat

The breed's long, flowing coat has a silky texture and drapes smoothly over the body contours beneath it. This is a true silk coat, single layered with no undercoat. It should not be thin, sparse, or "see through," nor should it be wooly, curly, or heavy enough to stand away from the body. The hair should be straight and can grow long enough to reach the ground. Pure white color, the breed's most distinguishing trait, is preferred in the show ring, but slight tan or lemon markings on the ears are permitted.

Head

Along with coat, color, and size, the Maltese is famed for his delightful expression. Several traits are responsible for creating this look.

The skull must be slightly rounded but never round enough to look domed or apple headed (like a Chihuahua) or flat (like a terrier).

Dramatically contrasted against the white coat, the dark Maltese eyes are definitely the breed's most striking facial feature. This gentle-spirited expression is produced by a combination of round eye shape, dark eye color, and black eye rims. Eyes should be medium sized.

Maltese ears also contribute to this elegant look by softly framing the head to accent the face. They should be set low, hang very close to the head, and be heavily covered with hair.

The pigment of the nose, lips, and eye rims should always be black. Eye rims may fade in winter but should regain their normal coloration after some sun exposure.

Maltese

The muzzle is of medium length and delicately tapered, never squared, boxy, or pointed. It should not slope down or tilt upward. The lips should fit closely over the teeth, which are set in a scissors (upper teeth closely overlap bottom teeth) or level bite (top and bottom teeth meet edge to edge).

The Maltese head is carried high atop a graceful neck. The neck should be long enough to create an elegant picture, positioning the head well above and in front of the body. If the neck is overly long and spindly or too short, the dog will look drastically out of proportion.

Body

Don't get the idea that looks are the whole story. Although this is a delicate, refined miniature breed, the Maltese is sturdy and athletic. Correct structure and proportion are just as important as coat and expression.

Rectangular proportions enhance the breed's natural agility. Strength and stamina are augmented by a deep, oval-shaped ribcage, which provides plenty of lung and heart room. The brisket (chest) extends to the elbow and tapers slightly, creating a definite waistline. The Maltese is actually slightly longer than tall, but his high tail set and carriage create the illusion of a shorter back and square outline. The tail should be covered by long hair and should extend smoothly off the back, curving over the body and lying against the side. It should never be carried straight up (like a Beagle's tail) or too high to touch the back (known as "flag" or "gay" tail) or flat over the back or tightly curled (like a Pug's tail). Maltese temperament sis reflected in this happy, confident tail carriage.

Correct gait is brisk, smooth, and self-assured, characterized by strong, rapid strides and an alert head and tail carriage. A Maltese should never move in a stiff or choppy manner or show signs of hopping or limping. On the move, the back should always be level, never sloping, bouncing, roaching (arching), or dipping. The legs are straight, fine boned, and well covered by the coat. The feet are small, compact, and rounded, with black footpads.

Temperament

The Maltese is first and foremost a companion. Their natural playfulness and liveliness virtually guarantee that your company will be entertained. Although loyal and fearless, they are not aggressive and should never act shy or defensive. They do, however, make excellent alarm dogs. They can be relied on to alert you to intruders, but they are not prone to excessive barking.

Maltese are intensely affectionate, and plenty of human contact is essential to their well-being. Ensuring

The Maltese is famed for his delightful expression.

Sleeping Arrangements

Dogs are pack animals and prefer to sleep near their pack leader. This doesn't imply that they cannot adjust to sleeping alone. If you want your Maltese to sleep in a crate or dog bed, stick to this routine from the beginning. Don't make the mistake of allowing the dog in bed "just for one night." If you do, plan to live with the consequences.

Plenty of dog owners allow their dogs to sleep in bed. There is nothing wrong with it, but once you do permit it, it's not an easy habit to reverse. Just keep a couple of things in mind.

If your puppy is not housetrained, be prepared to frequently get up for potty breaks during the night. And a toy dog can be injured if you accidentally roll on him or knock him out of bed while you are sound asleep. Maltese have no problem navigating low furniture, but they should never be allowed to jump from high beds or off furniture onto wood or tile flooring. You can build or buy steps to give your pet safe access to high furniture. A throw rug also helps cushion their landing. Maltese are sturdy, but they are not Olympians!

In most cases, dog and owner work out a perfectly synchronized somnambulant routine within a few nights.

12

Maltese

this requirement generally does not pose a problem. On the other hand, because they are so sweet and appealing, owners may be reluctant to impose any type of discipline. There is nothing wrong with indulging your Maltese, but this should not extend to disregarding bad behavior. Like all dogs, Maltese need to understand boundaries and rules. Longtime breeder Vicki Fierheller of Four Halls Maltese offers this advice on training: "Many toy owners are hesitant to discipline their puppies because they are afraid they might hurt them. (They think they are fragile.) Discipline does not have to be rough or physical. Most puppies respond very well to a firm 'NO!'"

A verbal correction is sufficient to check any unwanted behavior. Harsher methods are unnecessary for this sensitive breed and may lead to other behavior problems.

Supervise interactions between your Maltese and children.

Children and Maltese

Children are inevitably attracted to cuddly little dogs, but good intentions don't always equal good results. Supervise all interactions carefully, especially for children less than six years old or if young puppies are involved. Puppies are fragile and can be injured if accidentally dropped or stepped on. "It is not recommended that Maltese puppies be sold to families with young children under seven years," says breeder Vicki Fierheller. "It's not that Maltese don't like children—they do—but young children and baby Maltese are a bad combination. A Maltese at 12 weeks only weighs about 2 pounds (.9 kg). I've seen too many instances where a young child will accidentally drop or step on a puppy with serious and possibly fatal consequences. They simply don't understand the possible dangers of picking up a puppy or running around it."

For older, more responsible children, a Maltese can make an excellent pet, although precautions are still in order. A successful relationship is built on mutual respect and supervision. One of the most important things for a child to learn is that the safest way to pick up a small dog is to support his weight and hold him close to the body.

A child's attempts to pet, groom, or hold a Maltese can be frightening unless she has been shown the proper ways to do this. A fearful dog can resort to snapping or biting in self-defense. And even the most well-tempered dog will eventually object to rough handling or teasing.

The Stuff of
Everyday Life

Regardless of whether you are getting a puppy or an adult Maltese, find out exactly what supplies you will need and have them on hand before your new dog arrives. This will make the transition much easier for both of you.

Dog care essentials can be purchased from pet shops, mail order catalogs, or online retailers. Stick to products that are recommended for toy breeds or Maltese specifically. Selecting the right equipment rather than resorting to trial and error experimentation will save a lot of time, money, and confusion. If possible, get breeders' recommendations and hands-on demonstration for grooming products. Using the wrong products or using them improperly can result in a grooming nightmare. (See Chapter 4.)

Bedding

You'll need an assortment of washable bedding, like artificial sheepskin or quilted crate pads. Many toy dogs love to burrow into sleeping bag-type beds or curl up in donut beds. Whatever you choose, make sure that it's washable and fits into your washing machine without causing a meltdown. Satin beds are the preferred choice for Maltese in show coat because they won't tangle coats or build up static electricity, which can break hair tips.

All bedding should be tightly stitched to ensure that edges don't unravel, because loose threads can tangle in your dog's coat or around his legs. Maltese are not destructive, but avoid foam kapok filled pillows. Puppies may

be tempted to ingest loose stuffing poking through frayed seams or small tears. Wood and wicker beds are also a bad idea for the same reason. They look nice but are difficult to keep clean and dangerous if chewed. Molded plastic beds that can be frequently wiped down and disinfected are a better choice for puppies.

Cleaning Supplies

If you are bringing home a puppy, don't stint on cleaning supplies. Housetraining pads, disinfectants, and enzyme odor neutralizers are essentials for a puppy who's not yet housetrained. Maltese breeders use rolls of white newsprint

Maltese

Satin beds are the preferred choice for Maltese in show coat because they won't tangle coats.

paper for housetraining, which avoids the problem of black newsprint rubbing onto white coats. Pre-moistened puppy wipes to spot clean feet and faces and can be used to clean a variety of other things.

Collar and Lead

Toy-sized collars and leads (leashes) can be difficult to find, but they are essential. You cannot use heavy, bulky equipment on fragile toy dogs. Keep in mind that the size, weight, and design of clips, snaps, and buckles are just as important as the width and weight of collars and leads.

Collar

Collars should be narrow, 3/8 to 5/8 inches (.9 to 1.5 cm) wide, and made of flat, lightweight nylon or leather with no rough seams. A buckle collar with a small lightweight buckle is the best choice. A cat collar also works if you can't find an appropriately sized dog collar. When buckled, it should be snug enough to prevent the dog from slipping his head out or getting a leg caught in the collar but not uncomfortably tight. You should be able to slip two fingers inside of it, and it should be wide enough to protect your dog's throat. Collars of very narrow widths can be sharp. Do a comfort test by wrapping it around your wrist and giving it a good tug.

The collar should be accessorized with a toy-sized ID tag. If you can't find one small enough for a Maltese, your contact information can be embroidered or painted onto the collar.

FAMILY-FRIENDLY TIP

Who Is Responsible?

Dogs are often acquired for children as a companion, as a reward, or as a means of teaching them responsibility. These are good reasons, and children should be encouraged to help out with the dog's daily care. However, an adult must ultimately be responsible for supervising pet care. Regardless of a child's interest, her contribution must be geared toward her level of skill and maturity. For instance, Maltese grooming is something that cannot be neglected or done improperly. Also, well-intentioned children may forget to feed or walk a puppy, which will wreak havoc with training and housetraining routines. Underfeeding, overfeeding, and excessive or inappropriate treats can all result from a child's lack of judgment.

Children must understand the importance of dog training rules. If a dog is not permitted to jump on furniture or eat at the table, for example, the child should help to reinforce these rules. Otherwise, the dog will become hopelessly confused by mixed messages. More importantly, even the most devoted child cannot be relied on to notice subtle physical or behavioral changes that may signal the onset of illness.

Maltese

> *A flat buckle collar is best for your Maltese.*

Lead

Look for a lightweight nylon or leather lead 5/8 inch (1.5 cm) wide and no more than 6 feet (1.8 m) long with a small swivel snap. Retractable "flexi" leads are often too heavy and can be dangerous when walking small dogs in public places. Commonplace encounters that would not pose a hazard for larger dogs can be perilous for toy breeds. These can range from loose dogs, belligerent wildlife, kids on rollerblades, or open manholes. A very long lead makes it much more difficult to keep an eye on your dog or "reel him in" quickly when you encounter a dangerous situation.

Harness

Harnesses have become a popular alternative to collars, especially for toy breeds, and many puppies accept them more easily. If you choose to use a harness for your Maltese, keep these points in mind:

- Proper fit is crucial. This is generally calibrated by measuring around the widest point of the chest (behind the elbows) and adding 2 inches (5.1 cm). However, this is not foolproof because of the great variation in harness designs. It is best to try the harness on your dog and make sure it fits comfortably, allowing free range of motion and no chafing. Make sure that there are no rough seams or edges that might rub against his chest or neck—especially right behind the elbows.
- A harness does not provide the delicate control that can be achieved with a collar. This may cause your dog to get into the habit of pulling on the leash. Many dogs are prone to an "opposition reflex" and instinctively pull in the other direction when they feel the restraint of a harness.
- Most importantly, never leave the harness on your Maltese between walks. It may restrict his normal gait or cause skin irritations or coat tangles.

Crate

One of the most important doggy accessories you'll need is a crate. You will be using it to transport your pet during car trips, such as to the vet and to grooming appointments. It's also indispensable during housetraining and for times when you must leave your

Maltese unsupervised.

The most popular design for toy dogs is a small molded plastic or fiberglass crate. These are inexpensive, lightweight, and easy to carry and clean. Open-sided wire crates, which can be folded for storage, also work fine. Collapsible plastic crates are not recommended. Many dogs learn how to open these from the inside or accidentally collapse them onto themselves trying. Soft-sided mesh crates should only be used for dogs who are already crate trained. Any dog, even a small Maltese puppy, can escape from this type of crate if he decides to try.

The crate should be large enough for your dog to stand and turn around, approximately 4 inches (10.2 cm)

The Expert Knows

Licensing Your Dog

Many cities and towns require dogs to be licensed. The licensing process usually includes filling out a form, paying a small fee, and showing proof that your dog is vaccinated against rabies. Your dog must wear his license tag on his collar at all times. If he becomes lost, the tag number can provide another means of tracing his owner. Contact your city hall or animal control agency to find out dog ownership rules and restrictions in your locality *before* you acquire your dog. This ensures that you don't inadvertently violate any laws. It also pays to be familiar with your legal rights in case anyone decides to complain about your dog.

higher than the dog's height. An adult-sized crate may be too large for a puppy. An overly large crate is dangerous for travel and will totally defeat the purpose for housetraining.

Food and Water Bowls

You will need a couple of small, shallow, no-tip bowls for food and water. Stainless steel or ceramic dishes are durable and easy to clean. Plastic dishes have been known to aggravate tearstain problems in some Maltese.

Gate

No matter where you live, safety gates are essential for small breeds. When you first bring your dog home, you will need to restrict his access to some parts of your living space for training *and* for safety. A barrier will keep him from falling down stairs, off decks, out of windows, or into pools and hot tubs. It will also keep him out of potentially hazardous rooms in your house. He should not be allowed in any room that has not been "puppy proofed."

A temporary puppy pen can be assembled from "baby units"—interlocking panels available at baby stores. Pressure-mounted doorway baby gates are good for temporarily restricting access to certain parts of the house.

As you can see, there are plenty of canine barriers from which to choose. Just remember that when selecting canine exercise pens and gates, you must make sure that the bars are spaced closely enough to prevent a puppy from squeezing

20

Maltese

SENIOR DOG TIP

Transitions

Some breeds have a difficult time transitioning to a new home. Happily, this is not the case for Maltese. An adult will often adapt more easily to a new home because he is already socialized, trained, and accustomed to basic grooming. However, all dogs need time to adapt to major changes in their environment and routine. If possible, provide a crate, blanket, or a couple of toys that the dog is already familiar with to make him more comfortable.

Try to stick to the dog's previous regular feeding and exercise schedule. Make sure that he is eating, drinking, and eliminating normally. Don't switch foods and use bottled water at first, gradually mixing it with tap water for the first few days. The fact that a dog is housetrained does not rule out the possibility of training lapses. He cannot be expected to know when or where he should eliminate unless you clearly and consistently communicate the rules. Don't change the dog's name, and make sure that he wears an ID tag.

Exercise him only on lead or in a fenced area until you are certain he will come when called. Even if your yard is securely fenced, supervise him closely for the first few days. Toy dogs can squeeze through amazingly tiny gaps in fencing. If he is not accustomed to children or other pets, make introductions gradual. Don't overwhelm him. Given time and plenty of encouragement, most dogs soon acclimate to a new home and bond with new owners.

through or getting a foot or jaw stuck between the bars. Also, make sure that there are no rough or protruding edges that might catch or tear his coat.

"Going Out" Supplies

If you plan to take your Maltese walking on public streets, you will need a pooper scooper or clean-up bag. A lightweight pet carrier, backpack dog carrier, or pet stroller is also handy when taking your dog out. Because Maltese are single coated, your dog may also need a warm coat in cold weather.

Identification

No matter how careful you are, every dog is at risk of getting lost. Proper identification information is your best hope of finding your dog if this should happen to him. Common forms of identification include tattoos, microchips, and ID tags.

A small tattoo, usually done on the inside of the thigh, is permanent and non-invasive. The disadvantage is that tattoos can fade and become illegible after a few years.

Microchips, tiny chips implanted under the skin, have gradually become the favored form of permanent ID. The implantation procedure is quick and painless, comparable to a vaccination. The chip is usually implanted between the shoulder blades and read by a scanner.

An ID tag with your phone number is always a good supplement to a

Have some fun toys for your Maltese to play with.

tattoo or microchip. It provides the most visible, immediate form of identification.

Toys

An interesting assortment of toys is the best way to stop unwanted chewing and keep your Maltese entertained. Some toys, like pressed rawhide and dental bones, are also good to prevent tartar buildup. Small latex, plush, and rawhide toys that might be chewed and swallowed easily by larger dogs are usually fine for Maltese. They generally take good care of their toys, but these playthings should be regularly inspected to make sure that there are no potentially dangerous loose parts. Sooner or later, even favorite toys must be replaced for safety.

The Stuff of Everyday Life

The Expert Knows

Setting Up a Daily Routine

A consistent daily routine is the most important tool you will use to acclimate a new dog to your home. It not only facilitates training, it encourages bonding and helps your dog to recognize you as his pack leader. The schedule should be realistic, convenient and accommodate your dog's needs. (Don't set up a "New Year's Resolution" type of routine that will be impossible to stick to.) Once you have settled on a workable arrangement, do not be tempted to vary it. This will only confuse your dog and undermine training.

Eating, sleeping, and eliminating are the overriding issues to be addressed. Daily exercise and grooming are also essential. Depending on the age of your Maltese, his routine might also include daily training and socialization. And of course, daily play sessions are always required. "Maltese love to play," says Maltese breeder Vicki Fierheller. "We often use old socks or squeaky toys. Teaching your Maltese to play fetch is a great way to exercise him. The trick is to set aside a

playtime session each day. The dog wi' really look forward to it. After each play session, put the toy away until the next time."

An adult Maltese may need two meals per day and two or three short outings and one long walk. Depending on h: age, a puppy might need to be fed four times and taken to his designated elimination spot ten or more times every day. "We feed our puppies two to three meals a day until about four months of age, then cut back to two," states Vicki. "It is better to serve a meal, leave it down for about 20 minutes, and then pick it up. Free feeding makes it hard to monitor how much a puppy is eating and can result in a fat adult. Once he is eight to ten months old, we cut back to one meal a day with a dog biscuit making up the other meal."

"Some owners seem to feel they must be with their puppy 24 hours a day. In fact, I suggest just the opposite. Go out and leave him for an hour or so. Do it every day, and vary the times and length o your absence" advises Maltese expert and breeder Vicki Fierheller.

Along with training and socialization, every dog must learn to spend time on his own. This is contrary to his normal pack instinct, and it doesn't come naturally. Therefore, it should be part of his regular schedule from the beginning, or you may find yourself coping with misbehavior or separation anxiety. This is important for adults as well as puppies and includes dog proofing his designated territory. Vicki points out some of the household dangers that puppy proofing should address. "Electrical outlets should be covered and electric cords safely stowed out of reach. Houseplants, medications, and cleaning supplies are all hazardous. Potential dangers that are easily overlooked include banisters in upper halls along stairways and surrounding elevated decks and porches. Maltese puppies can easily slip through most of these bars."

Your Maltese must have a comfortably sized safe area where he can be left unsupervised. This might be an exercise pen or a partitioned area of a bedroom or kitchen. Whatever you decide, give him access to water and his bed, and ensure that he has plenty of toys to keep him occupied in your absence.

If you work, you may need to hire some help in keeping this schedule. Professional services should never be used as a substitute for your time and attention, although dog walkers and doggy daycare programs can be invaluable to working owners. They help to reinforce training and socialization and can help to ease a new dog's adjustment to unfamiliar household routines.

Dog walkers range from full-time professionals to neighborhood freelancers. Whatever you choose, get references and ask plenty of questions before entrusting anyone with your pet. Among other things, make sure that the person has experience handling toy breeds. If she customarily walks dogs in groups, make sure that these are appropriately sized exercise companions for a Maltese. Be wary of walkers who exercise pets at off-lead dog parks—these can be risky for small breeds.

Doggy daycare can provide a great social outlet for your pet while you are at work. Some owners take their pet every day, while others prefer to drop their dog off a couple of times a week to play, or they rely on indoor daycare facilities for exercise during inclement weather. When selecting a daycare program for your Maltese, pay an advance visit to check out the premises and interview the staff. Daycare programs can range from an extra service offered by a training facility or grooming shop to deluxe programs complete with swimming pools and webcams. In either case, the premises should be scrupulously clean, securely fenced, and adequately staffed by professionals familiar with the requirements of small breeds. Even if toy breeds are exercised separately from larger dogs, a 20-pound (9.1-kg) Pug can easily bully a 4-pound (1.8-kg) Maltese. The staff should reliably assess dogs' suitability as playmates.

Before enrolling your dog, you may be asked for proof of vaccination or for a health certification from your vet. Also, make sure that toys or bedding are allowed before bringing these items to daycare. Additional tips about daycare can be found at www.doggiedirectory.com.

Chapter 3

Good Eating

Choosing a healthy and appealing diet for your Maltese is easier said than done. Not only are you confronted with a million choices, but there is no end to the often contradictory expert advice on the subject. The key to unraveling the secret of canine nutrition is balance, and the deficiencies of an unbalanced diet cannot be corrected by overfeeding. Also, keep in mind that the healthiest diet will do no good if your dog refuses to eat it.

ost likely, you received information on diet when you acquired your Maltese. Breeders make these recommendations based on years of successfully raising generations of dogs, so don't be tempted to disregard it. Barbara Bergquist, breeder of 149 Su-Le Maltese champions since 1967, offers this advice on feeding and nutrition: "If you feed well-balanced, commercially prepared, top-quality dog foods, you can't go wrong. Breeders will feed their puppies and adults foods that they personally feel are the best for their dogs, and a buyer should continue with the exact diet that the puppy is accustomed to. A breeder should provide the names of the foods the dog is eating or a week's supply of it, and a wise owner will continue with the same food. If you or your vet deems it necessary to change the puppy's diet do it *gradually* by mixing some of the old food with the new brand over a two-week period, but *never* feed table scraps."

Casually experimenting with your dog's diet can result in health and behavior problems. Your dog's health, appearance, and energy level should be your guide. Sparkling eyes, a shiny coat, healthy skin, lots of energy, and the proper weight will confirm that your dog's diet is balanced and nutritious.

Commercial Foods

"A good commercial food promotes a good coat, strong bones, and a healthier, happier dog," says Barbara. "Maltese really aren't born 'picky eaters' but are made that way by offering too many variations in the diet."

All commercial dog foods contain a combination of meat and grain. Dogs require some carbohydrates in their diet, but they don't digest complex carbohydrates very efficiently, and nutrients derived from proteins and grains are not metabolized equally well. Meat-based foods provide

FAMILY-FRIENDLY TIP

Helping Out

Mealtime is one of the most enjoyable parts of a dog's daily routine for both dog and owner. Feeding the dog encourages bonding and can be a great way to promote a child's sense of responsibility toward a pet. Entrusting a child with this aspect of care will depend on her age and level of maturity. It's not exactly rocket science, but feeding the right amount of the right food at the right time makes a big difference in a dog's condition and behavior.

Children under six years of age might help by making sure the dog's water bowl is filled. Older children might be asked to give the dog his food once it's prepared and make sure that he eats it. Children should also understand that they are not permitted to tease or interrupt a dog while eating.

higher quality, more easily assimilated protein. Grain-based diets are less expensive, but they can lead to dietary deficiencies, especially in growing puppies. Whatever type or brand you choose, select a well-known company rather than a generic one.

One advantage to owning a small dog is that they don't eat a lot, so there is no reason to skimp on quality. The best choice is a premium commercial brand that has been thoroughly tested (preferably) in feeding trials and guaranteed to meet the basic nutritional standards for growth, maintenance, high performance, etc. The nutrient profile on the label should include an AAFCO (Association of American Feed Control Officials) guarantee.

Foods with comparable nutritional levels can differ drastically in taste and digestibility. The fact that a food contains specific amounts of proteins, carbohydrates, and fats doesn't guarantee that it is readily digestible. The "guaranteed analysis" printed on the label states the minimum amount of crude fat and protein and the maximum amount of crude fiber, ash, and moisture, but they can come from a wide range of sources. Understanding how to read the label is the best way to ensure that you are getting a quality commercial food.

Reading Food Labels

Interpreting a dog food label can seem like deciphering the Rosetta Stone. Every label includes reassuring claims that the food is balanced, complete, and mouthwatering. There are ways to figure out how true this is.

AAFCO-guaranteed formulas must meet basic nutritional levels. For instance, growth formulas are designed to meet nutritional requirements for growing puppies and must contain relatively higher percentages of fat and protein to sustain normal growth rates. The AAFCO requires a minimum of 22% protein for puppy foods. (Some brands may contain as much as 25% proteins and 17% fat.) Adult maintenance diets must contain at least 18% protein and 5% fat.

The ingredients of each formula are listed in descending order based on the relative percentage of

Commercial foods are usually the most convenient diet for your dog.

Maltese

To ensure that you're feeding a high-quality food, learn how to read commercial food labels.

each. The top ingredients should be predominantly meat rather than some type of cereal.

Check the sources of each ingredient. A high-protein food could be made from a plant- or animal-derived protein source, which makes a big difference in how much of this protein is actually nutritionally accessible.

The sources of meat ingredients also make a difference—and these should be specified. Meat, meat by-products, meat meal, and meat-flavored foods contain very different components. If a food is advertised as "turduckin," be sure that the label says "turduckin dog food." Foods with names like "turduckin flavor," "turduckin dinner," or "with turduckin" may actually contain very little turduckin. Avoid foods containing meal

or by-products, which are generally lower quality and made from less desirable sources like skin, organs, fatty tissue, feet, or heads.

Choose whole grains rather than grain by-products. Cereal ingredients can come from a rice, wheat, or corn, or less commonly, barley, potato, or a range of fruits and vegetables. Many breeders recommend avoiding formulas that contain soy.

Dry foods contain preservatives, but try to stay away from brands with large amounts of artificial colors, sweeteners, or chemical preservatives. Some are naturally preserved with vitamin E or C. Even foods with preservatives will become rancid and lose nutritional value after about three months, so check the expiration date, and don't buy too much at one time.

Types of Commercial Food

The most common types of commercial food are canned, dry, and semi-moist.

Canned Food

For small breeds, like Maltese, canned foods are the most popular. Several brands are formulated specifically for toys, packaged in convenient toy-sized containers. The advantages of canned foods are that they are high-grade sources of protein, provide a great variety of flavors and textures, have a long shelf life, and taste delicious. On the other hand, canned food is more expensive and contains a high percentage of water. You are not only paying for a lot of water, but a small dog must consume proportionally more of it to meet his nutritional requirements. Canned foods usually don't contain artificial preservatives, but they will spoil quickly if not consumed soon after serving.

Dry Food

Dry foods, also known as kibble, are convenient to store and to feed. Although not available in quite as much variety as canned foods, most companies now market special formulas for toy breeds. These are made of smaller sized kibble, with concentrated amounts of nutrients per serving. Dry foods are more economical and will keep for about three months once opened. Many dogs enjoy the crunchy texture, which can contribute to a dog's dental hygiene.

Dry foods contain proportionally more fiber and carbohydrates and often lower grade types of protein

SENIOR DOG TIP

Feeding the Older Dog

Older dogs are more reluctant to accept change and may reject an unfamiliar food, so don't change your dog's diet unless you must. If you notice a sudden change in your dog's weight, check with your vet to rule out any underlying health problem. An older, sedentary Maltese may need a senior dog or weight control formula. Weakness, pain, or underlying illness can undermine appetite and set the stage for bigger health issues. Reluctance to eat can also result from tooth decay. Elderly dogs may need softer foods and more time to eat their usual amount. Splitting daily rations into two or three smaller meals may encourage better eating habits.

Prescription diets are commonly recommended for specific health disorders. Many dogs are reluctant to eat these, and convincing them otherwise can take some ingenuity. Warming the food and soaking it in broth can help.

Good Eating

than canned foods. They also don't have the taste appeal of canned foods, and many owners combine canned and dry foods to compensate for this. You can also try mixing dry food with a couple spoonfuls of cottage cheese, lean cooked beef, or broth.

Semi-Moist

Semi-moist foods are designed to combine the palatability of canned food and the convenience of dry food. They are available in single-serving packages and will not spoil quickly once opened. However, they contain large amounts of fillers, sweeteners, and artificial preservatives. Most of them are designed to look like hamburger or chunks of beef, thanks to generous additions of red food dye. Foods containing dyes can discolor your dog's facial hair, increase problems with tear staining, or trigger food allergies.

Noncommercial Diets

No commercial diet is perfect for every dog, and there is no way to completely monitor the ingredients of a commercially prepared food. The only way to precisely control your dog's diet is to prepare your own dog food.

Home-Cooked Diet

Despite decades of advice from veterinarians and canine nutritionists, most owners continue to supplement their dog's diet with table scraps, snacks, and treats. Dogs enjoy a bit of variety in their diet, and in moderation, it is fine. However, as breeder Barbara Bergquist points out, "Overdoing this can lead to a lifetime of feeding problems. Any breed can become a picky eater if 'people' foods are fed rather than a good diet specifically made for dogs. A lot of first-time dog owners fall into this pit, and often there is no alternative but to continue feeding dog food mixed with people food."

It's possible to prepare your own dog food, but don't make the mistake of assuming that a dish of table scraps is comparable to a well-balanced homemade diet. Dogs are omnivorous and not designed to thrive on a vegetarian diet, so a homemade diet must include meat, adequate amounts of essential fatty acids, easily digestible

Maltese

carbohydrates, and a proper vitamin/ mineral balance. Over time, even a slight imbalance can result in long-term health effects. "Homemade diets or raw diets can be fine," notes longtime Maltese breeder Vicki Fierheller, "but it must be balanced nutritionally. If you go that route, please talk to your vet or nutritionist first." A homemade diet should be supplemented to prevent possible vitamin deficiencies.

There are some advantages to feeding your Maltese a homemade diet. Dogs definitely prefer home-cooked food, and you will know exactly what he is eating.

This can be especially important for pets with food allergies.

Preparation is time consuming and even for a small dog, it will be more expensive. There are scores of books and websites offering recipes and advice on how to prepare nutritionally complete homemade diets for your dog.

Raw Diet

The trendiest type of homemade diet is unquestionably the raw food diet. In the last decade, these have become increasingly popular with pet owners and breeders and have garnered endorsements from many pet care professionals. Advocates point out that commercial dog foods are "unnatural" in that they are highly processed and often contain artificial colorings, preservatives, and inferior-grade ingredients. These dietary shortcomings have been implicated in a wide range of chronic health and behavior problems.

Raw diets attempt to recreate the typical feeding regime of the ancestral canine, mainly raw bones, meat, and chicken. The benefits range from cleaner teeth to better behavior. However, you should keep a few things in mind before giving it a try. "Some breeders feed a raw diet," says Barbara. "I won't comment except to say that I personally

A homemade diet is often prescribed for dogs with food allergies.

Food Allergies

Food allergies or sensitivities can cause symptoms ranging from repeated digestive upsets, chronic skin irritations, or severe respiratory distress.

It is possible for a dog to become allergic to a food that he has eaten regularly in the past. Ingredients most often implicated in allergic reactions are horse meat, beef, pork, lamb, poultry, eggs, dairy products (these include yogurt and cottage cheese, as well as milk), corn, soy, and various food additives. Treats or chews can also be culprits.

Consult your vet or a specialist for a definitive diagnosis if you suspect that your Maltese is suffering from a food allergy. In order to rule out each suspected food, you must place your Maltese on an elimination diet supervised by your vet.

Once you have discovered the offending ingredient, you will need to change diets. Many breeders recommend foods containing rice or potato for dogs with food allergies. Exotic proteins like rabbit, elk, or whitefish are also less likely to trigger food allergies.

When changing foods, watch for changes in coat, condition, and weight. It may take up to six weeks for an allergic reaction to become evident or to begin to subside.

Maltese

want my meat cooked before I eat it to at least kill any contamination or parasites it may harbor, and I want no less for my dogs." Raw meat can be a source of parasites and *Salmonella* and *E.coli* bacteria. Infections that might be insignificant in a large dog can quickly turn serious in a small breed like the Maltese. Infected dogs can also become carriers.

Dogs are natural scavengers who normally consume a wide variety of meats, grains, and vegetables. High-protein raw diets consisting entirely of raw beef or chicken are not balanced and can lead to nutritional deficiencies.

Feeding a raw diet is also very messy. You will need to thoroughly clean your dog's eating area after each meal to prevent possible bacterial contamination. Your long-coated, short-muzzled Maltese may need to be bathed after every meal. Also, although canine teeth are designed for meat eating, small breeds may not have enough jaw power to chew bones or large meat chunks, which may lead to choking or intestinal obstruction.

When to Feed

You'll need to decide if you're going to free feed your Maltese (leave food out all day), feed him on a schedule, or have a combination of both. Keep in mind that unlike free feedings, scheduled feedings not only discourage picky eating habits, but they help to prevent obesity. Breeder Barbara Bergquist's feeding routine includes a combination of scheduled meals and free feeding.

"I leave a dish of dry food out for them at all times. Most will crunch a few pieces of the dry, making for cleaner teeth. Often they will wean themselves off the moist food to an all-dry kibble diet. Personally, I feed a good commercial canned food in the morning and evening, and of course they have access to the dry whenever they feel hungry."

Regular scheduled mealtimes will go a long way toward instilling a good appetite and good eating habits. As Pavlov proved in his famous experiments, dogs become conditioned to feel hungry as mealtime approaches. Your Maltese will be far less likely to eat poorly or dawdle over his dinner if he knows that it's going to be served and taken away at specific times.

Maltese are not typically voracious eaters and may need a longer time to consume a normal portion. There is nothing wrong with that, but uneaten food should be picked up after 20 minutes.

Puppies need to be fed more often than adult dogs.

Age-Appropriate Feeding

Good
Dog

eeder Barbara Bergquist advises, "Maltese require three to four small meals a day as pups and tw
eals a day as adults." Regardless of the instructions on the dog food package, your dog's conditio
ould be your ultimate guide. Suggested amounts tell you approximately how much your dog shou
nsume. Because of variations in metabolism, though, dogs of the same weight may need more or
ss. Likewise, portions may need to be increased or decreased depending on your dog's activity lev
t into the habit of regularly evaluating your dog's condition and moderate his portions before th
tuation gets out of control.

Young puppies are normally fat and shapeless. By four months of age, they should begin to
velop adult body contours. When you place your hand across your dog's back, you should be able
nd his ribs, not a padding of fat. When looking down at your Maltese, some indication of a waist
ould be visible. If not, he is getting too fat. If his ribs and hip bones can be easily seen through
at, he is too thin.

It's not unusual for puppies to temporarily lose their appetite during teething, which takes pla
tween four and six months of age. It may help to feed softer foods until the teething is complete

Sample Feeding Schedule for Each Phase of Your Dog's Life

Age	Times per Day	Amount	Best Food
Puppies (8-12 weeks)	Four	1/4-1/2 cup (59-118ml)	Growth formula
Adolescents (3-6 months)	Three	1/4-1/2 cup (59-118ml)	Growth formula
Active Adults (6 months-7 years)	Two	1/4-1/2 cup (59-118ml)	Adult, toy breed/maintenance
Sedenary Adults (up to 7 years)	Two	1/4-1/2 cup (59-118ml)	Adult, toy breed/maintenance
Seniors (9 plus years)	Two	1/4-1/2 cup (59-118ml)	Senior or growth depending on dog's needs

Obesity

Our national obsession with diet and weight has not carried over to our pets. Obesity has become the number-one nutritional disorder afflicting America's pets. Most dog owners tend to worry if their pet is eating enough and perceive a roly-poly body as a sign of good health.

An occasional treat is fine, but don't be guilty of killing your Maltese with kindness. Excess weight increases your dog's risk for back and joint problems, pancreatitis, heart problems, and diabetes. All these things spell a shorter, less happy life. A Maltese should not weigh more than 7 pounds (3.1 kg), and pets don't become obese without their owners' assistance! Not surprisingly, the prime culprit is snacking between meals. "If they are fed too much human food, Maltese tend to gain more weight than they should," notes Barbara. "Excess weight is not good for the heart or for their small bone structure."

Just like junk food, snacks and treats tend to be irresistible because of their high fat and calorie content. It's easy to overlook the cumulative effects of a few indiscretions; a handful of dog biscuits may seem harmless, for example, but for a Maltese, it's the equivalent of eating an entire pizza. "I can't stress enough the importance of making sure that your pet maintains the correct weight. Maltese can become overweight very easily, particularly if they are fed scraps and tidbits. You should be able to run your fingers along the ribs and just be able to feel them. If you can't feel anything but fat, then your dog needs to go on a diet!" emphasizes Vicki.

If your veterinarian has pronounced your Maltese overweight, the problem should be tackled with a combination of diet and exercise (both done under her supervision). Your first step is to cut out the snacks. Switch to a weight-reduction food or substitute low-calorie rice cakes, popcorn, or cooked vegetables for half of your dog's normal ration. If he is seriously out of condition, start by lengthening his daily walks and gradually build up to a more challenging shape-up routine.

Table Manners

Good table manners should be incorporated into your dog's training routine.

An occasional treat is fine, but keep an eye on your Maltese's weight.

Foods to Avoid

Some foods really are toxic and should never be given to your Maltese, such as chocolate, onions, and foods containing the artificial sweetener xylitol. Caffeine and alcohol are also on the forbidden list. If you offer your Maltese table food, avoid anything spicy or greasy. Never give small bones, raw or cooked. All treats should be offered in tiny bite-sized pieces to prevent choking.

Preventing bad table manners is simple—just don't encourage them to start with. Your Maltese will quickly learn to eat his meals in a certain place at a special time without expecting to join you at dinner hour.

Begging at the table is one of the most difficult habits to revise. Puppies are instinctively "wired" to beg for food from dominant pack members. They learn this from their mother during weaning, and well-meaning owners often reinforce it. It's hard to resist giving your Maltese a taste. But doing so only encourages him to become more annoying and demanding every time you try to sit down to eat. It can also create a picky eater, because your dog is smart enough to know the difference between a lamb chop and a bowl of dog food. Breeder Barbara Bergquist recounts: "I have never had a picky eater except for my very first Maltese acquired 40 years ago. I created a monster. I started giving her meat from the table, and of course she then would avoid her dog food. It got to the point that if I cooked her chicken, she would turn her nose up and walk away muttering 'I wanted roast beef today.'" Barbara learned her lesson and has maintained generations of her top-winning Maltese on good-quality commercial diets since then.

Supplements

Maltese experience their major growth by four to five months of age and reach adult size by six or eight months. High levels of fat, protein, vitamins, and minerals may not be needed after that.

Unless your breeder or veterinarian specifically recommends supplements for your Maltese, don't use them. Excessive or improperly balanced supplements can do more harm than good by producing nutritional imbalances or vitamin toxicity. It's easy to overdose a small dog like a Maltese. Dietary supplements can also react with prescription medications.

If supplements are recommended for your Maltese, choose products made specifically for dogs, not humans. Look for CL (Consumer Lab) and USP (United States Pharmacopoeia) endorsements to guarantee product purity. Read the dosage instructions carefully.

For more information, visit the US Pharmacopeia's website at www.usp.org, or go to www. consumerreportsmedicalguide.org. The Natural Medicines Comprehensive Database (www.naturaldatabase.com) contains the most comprehensive information regarding safety, effectiveness, and possible drug interactions of 14,000 supplements.

Chapter 4

Looking Good

Maltese are known for their beautiful coats, but keeping that coat looking good takes time and money. "I tell anyone interested in buying a Maltese that if they are not prepared to deal with the coat on a daily basis (whether they keep it short or long), then the Maltese is not for them," states seasoned Maltese breeder Vicki Fierheller. Even if you intend to have your pet professionally groomed, this must be supplemented with daily care. Maintaining a regular grooming routine amounts to far less work than dealing with a matted, dirty, stained coat. This isn't simply a cosmetic problem. Neglecting your dog's grooming will impact his health and temperament.

B
e prepared to invest time, work, *and* money into keeping your Maltese presentable. Discount grooming supplies may save you a bit of the latter but will add to the time and work involved.

Grooming Supplies for Your Maltese

If possible, purchase your grooming equipment from a source that specializes in products for long-haired or "drop-coated" breeds. Not only are these designed especially for Maltese coats, the sales staff is usually happy to offer expert recommendations and advice on coat care.

You need a slicker brush for coats maintained in a puppy clip, a pin brush (without the plastic balls on the end) for long coats, a metal comb with wide and closely spaced teeth to check the coat for snags, a flea comb for combing debris from under the eyes, spray-on detangler, and spray-on conditioner to reduce static while brushing. Also, select a shampoo and conditioner specifically for long-coated dogs. Some formulas contain coat whiteners, which is a bonus. Pre-moistened wipes, eye-cleaning solutions, or cornstarch are good for controlling tearstains. If you are using cornstarch, you will need a small make-up brush to apply it. A doggy toothbrush and toothpaste are essential as well. For foot care, you need a small nail clipper, small, blunt-tipped scissors, and a good-quality pair of trimming shears. Bows are not required, but topknots are the most common way

Maltese

Is a Grooming Table Necessary?

A good grooming table is a valuable investment. You will find yourself using it to simplify all sorts of grooming chores. They can be found in many styles and sizes, but sturdiness should be your main priority. Look for a design with legs set at the corners of the table, not close to the center—nothing will undermine table training more than a wobbly table. The top should be covered with a nonporous, nonskid surface that's easy to clean. If the top is ridged, the ridges should run across the width, not the length, of the tabletop. Otherwise, they won't do a thing to secure your dog's footing.

Many tables are fitted with a clamp or holder for a grooming arm, which can come in handy. The arm should fit tightly into the holder and easily adjust to the dog's height. Check this by giving the table and arm a good hard shake. A loosely attached grooming arm is extremely dangerous.

If you plan to groom your Maltese on a table, introduce him to this from a young age. Stand him on the table several times each day, and reward him with treats and praise. A positive attitude about the table also makes vet exams much easier.

Never leave your Maltese unattended on a grooming table.

to keep hair out of eyes and food. A stunning assortment of bows, bands, and clips are available from pet supply companies.

A grooming table with a non-skid surface and a freestanding hair dryer will definitely make life easier if you plan to do your own grooming.

Coat and Skin Care

The Maltese coat is classified as "silky," fine textured, nonshedding, and capable of growing quite long. Regardless of length, coats of this texture are prone to matting and break easily if not properly cared for. This is why the long coats of show dogs are protected by bands and wrappers. Maintaining a

Maltese with long show coats need their hair put in wrappers so that it doesn't break or mat.

Maltese coat in a short pet or puppy trim can minimize routine care. But regardless of length, dead hair must be brushed out of the coat regularly to prevent mats and tangles.

Brushing

Brushing must become a daily routine from the day your Maltese arrives. Even in a short puppy clip, the Maltese coat will tangle without daily grooming. Hair grows in cycles, and brushing removes dead hair and stimulates follicles to produce new growth. It improves circulation, distributes natural skin oils through the coat, and really does make your Maltese feel better.

You must brush your Maltese before you bathe him.

Looking Good

The coat must be brushed all over. To do this, your dog must lie cooperatively on his back or side as you groom him. Begin teaching your puppy to do this while he is young and accepting, and be sure to brush him consistently. Otherwise, it will be impossible to brush hard to reach spots that are especially prone to matting.

You will need a pin brush, a small slicker brush, a steel comb with wide and narrow teeth, a small "flea comb" with finely spaced teeth, and an anti-static coat spray.

Mist one area of the coat with conditioning/anti-static spray, and brush one section at a time with your pin brush. Brush against the lay of the coat from skin to hair tip. Be careful working around the ears and face. It may be easier to use a smaller brush and comb for these areas. You may prefer a small slicker brush for legs and feet.

Once you have gone over the entire coat, brush through it again with the dog standing so that the hair falls into its normal position. Finish by combing the entire coat to make sure that you have not missed any tangles.

Dealing With Mats

If you find a mat, saturate it with detangling spray or cornstarch, and begin gently pulling it apart with your fingers. Once you have loosened it as much as possible, use one tooth of your comb to unravel the tangled hairs

at the edge, and smooth those apart with the pin brush. Alternately, pick it apart with the comb and smooth it with the brush. Don't cut it or pull it.

Dematting is a painstaking process. Vicki offers this final advice on the subject of matted coats. "If the tangles get ahead of you, take your dog to a groomer. Don't wait until the dog is such a tangled mess that the only recourse is for the groomer to shave him down."

Topknots

Tying the head hair up into two symmetrically placed bows (topknots) is the classic Maltese hairstyle. It looks great, but it's not mandatory. Hair can be kept out of the eyes by trimming it, braiding it, or using hair clips.

If you want to keep your dog's hair in topknots, you'll need some practice, and your Maltese must be trained to accept them. Begin by putting his

Two topknots are traditional, but you can also tie a single topknot to keep the hair out of your Maltese's eyes.

Maltese

hair into a single topknot with a tiny rubber band. Some breeders use orthodontic bands, or you can purchase thin, breakaway bands from grooming supply shops. These are easier to remove, causing less hair breakage. Make sure that the hair isn't pulled too tight. Even if your dog agrees to leave his topknot in place, you must take it down and comb it out every day.

Bathing

Little furry white dogs require frequent bathing. Spot cleaning the feet and face can help somewhat, but your Maltese will probably require weekly bathing. Because it must be done so often, many owners opt to bathe their Maltese at home rather than making so many trips to the groomer.

Use only quality shampoos and conditioners for long-haired or drop-coated breeds. Human hair care products have a higher pH level and may dry or damage the coat. "If the owner chooses to bathe at home," warns Vicki, "that is fine, but it is very important that the dog *not* be bathed if tangled. Ever wash a wool sweater by mistake? Did you notice how it shrinks and becomes more dense? That is what happens to tangles when washed—they tighten up and become ten times more difficult to get out. So the cardinal grooming rule is to *never bathe a matted Maltese!*"

The Expert Knows

Haircuts

"Most pet owners do not keep their Maltese in a full coat," notes breeder Vicki Fierheller. "More commonly, they are kept in puppy cuts. Unless they are wallflowers, most Maltese go for daily walks, are out in the grass, and really live in their hair. It takes real dedication to keep a typically active Maltese in a semi- or full coat. If an owner wants to maintain look of a long coat with less work, she can trim the legs and belly coat short but leave the sides long." An alternative style is to keep the whiskers, ears, tail, and head coat long and the rest of the body coat trimmed to a couple of inches (cm) in length. "To keep a Maltese in a puppy clip, I suggest a visit to the groomer about every four to six weeks," says Vicki. "By then, even with home brushing, the dog will be due for a trim, bath, nail clipping, ear cleaning, etc."

A kitchen sink or laundry tub is just the right size to bathe a Maltese. Place a nonskid mat in the bottom and assemble all of your supplies, which include shampoo, conditioner, towel, grooming spray, comb, and hair dryer, before you put your dog in the tub. Saturate the entire coat with warm water. Gently massage the shampoo through the coat, one section at a time, from skin to hair tips. Don't scrub it into the coat or work it against the lay of the hair. Also, be careful not to get any soap in the eyes or water in the ears. You will need a spray attachment for rinsing, because it's almost impossible to completely rinse a long coat by pouring water over it. If you don't rinse out all the soap, skin irritation and coat damage could result.

Removing coat stains such as blood, urine, or grass can be challenging. Use a purple—not blue—coat-whitening shampoo and only lukewarm water to avoid setting the stains even more. Saturate the stained areas with shampoo, and leave it on for at least ten minutes before rinsing. It sometimes helps to saturate a small washcloth with purple shampoo and place this over the stain for a few minutes. Needless to say, don't try this technique for facial staining. It may require several treatments to completely remove heavy stains from a white coat.

Conditioner should be left on for a few minutes before the final rinse. Before removing your dog from the tub, gently squeeze excess water from the coat. Wrap him in a towel and blot as much moisture from his hair as possible. Don't rub because this will cause mats. After towel drying, apply a grooming spray, and comb it through with the wide teeth of the comb. Hair is more elastic but also more fragile when wet, sort of like wet spaghetti. Let your dog have a good shake, and then finish up with a hair dryer.

Drying

Small breeds like Maltese are prone to chilling after a bath. A dryer is the best way to quickly and thoroughly dry him all the way to the skin. Brushing the hair while drying it gives a nice straight finish to the coat. To do this, you will need a stand dryer and a grooming table. Set the dryer on low/warm, and test it on your hand to make sure that the temperature is comfortable. Never leave it on high or leave the dryer blowing on an unattended dog.

Familiarize your Maltese with the hair dryer while he is still a puppy. Otherwise, it will be hard to convince him to patiently tolerate the sound and sensation.

Dental Care

Maltese, like all toy breeds, require attentive dental hygiene to prevent tartar buildup and tooth loss. Train your puppy to have his mouth examined and his teeth cleaned as soon as you get him. This will save you

big vet bills and minimize the need for risky dental cleaning under anesthesia.

Dental plaque is a combination of saliva proteins mixed with bacteria and food debris. This sticky yellowish substance can be easily wiped off your dog's teeth with a doggy toothbrush or small gauze pad when it's first deposited. Use baking soda or canine toothpaste, not human toothpaste. If plaque is allowed to accumulate, it eventually hardens into dark brown tartar. This cannot be wiped off. It eventually works its way under the gum line, causing infection and destroying the roots of the teeth. This is when owners usually notice that their dog has developed really bad breath. The bacteria can also spread through the bloodstream, damaging major organs.

To brush your dog's teeth, you'll need a toothbrush or finger brush and doggy toothpaste. Many types of canine toothbrushes are available on the market, some made especially for toy breeds. You may need to experiment to discover what works best for your Maltese. For some dogs, a small, dampened gauze pad wrapped around your fingertip is most easily accepted. Either hold your dog on your lap or sit him on a grooming table. Gently open his lips, and brush each tooth in a circular motion. Talk to him and praise him while you work. Pay special attention to the gum line and spaces between the teeth. It is not necessary to clean the inside surface of each tooth, because the dog's tongue normally keeps this side free of debris. As you move toward the back teeth, you may need to work by touch. Regular brushing will remove any accumulation of soft plaque, but tartar buildup cannot be removed this way.

Tartar can only be removed with dental tools or an ultrasound scaler. Depending on the amount of buildup and your dog's attitude, this may need to be done under anesthesia. Some veterinarians offer dental cleaning without anesthesia, which is safer but still no fun for the dog.

Ear Care

Ears should be examined weekly. Dropped ears, which hang down against the side of the head, and a long coat can conceal a brewing ear problem until it turns into a serious

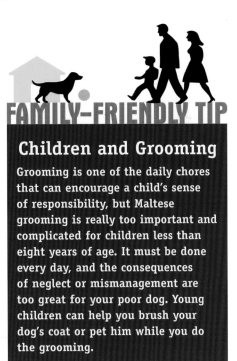

FAMILY-FRIENDLY TIP

Children and Grooming

Grooming is one of the daily chores that can encourage a child's sense of responsibility, but Maltese grooming is really too important and complicated for children less than eight years of age. It must be done every day, and the consequences of neglect or mismanagement are too great for your poor dog. Young children can help you brush your dog's coat or pet him while you do the grooming.

infection. Maltese ears should be pale pink on the inside. Head shaking or tilting, ear scratching, and odor all indicate a problem.

Ears should be cleaned every time you bathe your dog, more often if they seem irritated. Cleaning flushes out debris and creates an unfavorable pH environment for infections. Use a canine ear-cleaning solution or a 50/50 dilution of white vinegar and water. Never clean ears with peroxide or rubbing alcohol, which are too harsh for delicate ear tissue.

Hold the ear flap open, squeeze a few drops of solution into the ear, close the ear flap, and massage it into the ear canal for a few seconds. Use a cotton ball to wipe the ear opening and clean away any visible debris. Hold your dog's head firmly while doing this, and do not probe into the ear. Yellowish earwax is normal. If the ear canal looks inflamed or you find a lot of red or brown debris, visit your vet—your dog may be suffering from a yeast or bacterial infection or ear mites.

Excess hair growing in the ear canal can lead to infection. Remove it by plucking it with your fingers, tweezers, or forceps. Sprinkling ear powder into the ear helps get a better grip on the hair and makes it come out more easily. Pluck only a few hairs at a time, and apply an antiseptic ointment afterwards.

Another potential source of ear infections is moisture in the ear canal, so be careful not to get water in your dog's ears during a bath. Also, be sure to dry the ear thoroughly afterward.

Eye Care

Dogs normally accumulate debris in the corners of their eyes that must be removed daily. Gently wipe it away with a damp cloth or pre-moistened eye cleaning pad, or comb it out with a flea comb.

"Tear staining is always an issue with Maltese," admits breeder Vicki Fierheller, "so daily cleaning around the eyes is recommended." A tearstain is a reddish-brown discoloration of the hair under the eyes, around the muzzle, and sometimes on the feet. It is basically a cosmetic problem, but persistent dampness can lead to skin irritation or staph infection.

To stop the staining, you must find the cause. Irritated, watery eyes can be

Dental care is especially important in toy breeds.

Use Grooming Time Wisely

Get in the habit of giving your Maltese a quick exam to detect signs of illness, parasites, or minor injuries during daily grooming sessions. You will instantly recognize when something is wrong if you are totally familiar with your dog's normal health. The most important thing to check is his attitude, energy level, and responses. His eyes should be clear and bright, and his expression should be calm and alert. His breathing should be relaxed, regular, and quiet. He should not have objectionable breath or ear or skin odors. Run your hands down his body and legs, checking for stiffness, tenderness, or unusual lumps. His skin should be pale pink, supple, and warm, with no sign of redness, flaking, scratching, cuts, or bruises. His back should be strong, straight, relaxed, and flexible, and his belly should not feel tender, tense, or bloated. You should not notice any drastic changes in his weight. If anything seems amiss, don't hesitate to consult your vet. It may be nothing serious, but you can't be sure. Catching a minor problem in time can prevent it from turning into a serious health issue.

The time that you spend grooming your Maltese does more than make your dog look good. It can be a tremendous source of mutual enjoyment and fosters trust and communication. Grooming time is also good for your health because it lowers blood pressure, relieves stress, and boosts the immune system. Studies have shown that grooming activities stimulate the release of endorphins in the brain, creating a sense of well-being in both people and their dogs.

caused by obstructed tear ducts, temporary irritations like wind or pollen, allergies, or injuries. Less commonly, ear infections and dental problems, like teething, can cause secondary eye irritations. Foods or treats containing coloring or additives can lead to tearstaining as well. The mineral content of your water supply can also be a possible cause, so try switching to bottled or filtered water. Some breeders recommend putting a few drops of apple cider vinegar into a dog's water to reduce staining. Of course, that will only work if the dog drinks it!

Keep the stained areas as clean as possible. Daily applications of cornstarch or tearstain remover can help. Make sure that your dog's hair is kept out of his eyes. If his eyes appear irritated, try washing them out with artificial tears or eyewash.

Most vets prescribe oral antibiotics to treat tearstaining. It usually takes about three weeks to clear up the problem, but it can return when treatment stops. If broad-spectrum antibiotics don't help, your vet can culture the tear residue to identify which antibiotic works best.

Once you have dealt with the underlying cause, the staining will stop. But it will take several weeks for the hair to grow out in its normal white color.

Nail Care

Nail care is one of the most often neglected aspects of grooming, which can create plenty of problems for your dog. Round, compact Maltese feet can become permanently splayed and flattened by walking on overgrown nails. Nails can break easily or tear if caught in bedding, and they can cause eye injuries.

Feet and nails should be inspected weekly. Small injuries, debris lodged

SENIOR DOG TIP

Grooming the Older Dog

Older dogs typically relish the care and attention of grooming sessions, but you may need to revise a few things. Older dogs generally fare better in a pet trim. Grooming sessions should be kept short to minimize stress. Older dogs are also more prone to chilling, so more brushing and less bathing may work better.

Products that work fine for younger Maltese may not be best for seniors. Older dogs have thinner hair and more delicate skin. They can be more susceptible to dry skin, hot spots, or demodectic mange. Dry skin or a dry coat may benefit from a slightly oily coat conditioner. Footpads and noses may need an occasional application of vitamin E oil to prevent dryness.

Less active dogs may need their nails trimmed more frequently. Anal glands should be checked often to ensure that they don't become impacted. Teeth and gums should be inspected regularly as well.

Maltese

between toe pads, or broken nails can be easily missed if you don't take the time to check. Nails may need trimming every two to four weeks, depending on your dog's activity level.

Begin teaching your puppy to cooperate for foot inspection and nail trimming as soon as you get him. "Foot phobias" are rare in young puppies; it usually becomes an issue in adolescent dogs who have not been trained to accept it. If your Maltese doesn't like having his feet handled, you will have to revise this attitude. Be firm, gentle, and calm. Never turn feet handling into a confrontation. If your dog panics or resists, stop and try again the next day. But do it every day, and always praise him when he cooperates. Rewarding him with a favorite toy or tasty morsel will also go a long way toward encouraging a good attitude.

For Maltese pedicures, you need a scissors- or guillotine-type nail trimmer, clotting powder, and small, blunt-tipped scissors to trim excess hair between footpads.

Either stand your dog on a table or hold him on your lap to trim nails. White nails make it easier to see the "quick"—the vein running down the nail. Cutting the quick causes pain and bleeding. If your dog has some white and some dark nails, estimate the correct length by trimming the light ones first. Trim only the portion of the nail that extends past the quick. If your Maltese has dewclaws, tiny

rudimentary claws on the inside of the leg, front, back, or both, don't forget to trim those, too. They are easy to miss and will eventually grow all the way around and pierce the toepad.

If you accidentally trim a nail too short and cause bleeding, don't panic—it looks much worse than it is. Stick the entire nail into clotting powder until the bleeding stops. (Rinsing it with water will delay clotting.) If you don't have any clotting powder on hand, pack the bleeding nail with cornstarch, press it into a bar of soap, or apply pressure and ice until the bleeding stops. Don't let the dog to walk on it until you are sure that it is completely clotted.

Hair growing between the toepads should be trimmed to the pad. Don't try to trim between the toes. You can also neaten up the foot hair by rounding off long, uneven hair to the level of the footpads.

Begin teaching your puppy to cooperate for nail trimming as soon as you get him.

Chapter 5

Feeling Good

Because you spend so much time with your Maltese, you are naturally attuned to his normal state of health. This gives you a tremendous advantage in recognizing when something is wrong. Yes, your dog really can tell you when he is not feeling well. Keep in mind that you are the first line of defense in protecting his health.

Finding a Veterinarian

Hopefully, vet visits will be rare, but if your Maltese does suffer an accident or become seriously ill, you will need to have confidence in your vet. Finding the right one is not a casual endeavor.

The advantages of large clinics include multiple specialties and testing procedures in one location. The disadvantage may be impersonal service. You may see a different vet every visit. This won't be a problem if you choose a small practice. Your dog will get to know his vet, and the vet will be familiar with your dog's health history. You may also have to wait for test results that have been sent out to labs, or you may be referred to outside specialists for unusual problems.

Whether you prefer a large or small practice, the vet should be experienced in treating toy breeds. She must be comfortable handling them and be knowledgeable about their special needs. Toys react differently to stress, and their metabolic differences must be considered when administering anesthesia and vaccinations and calibrating drug dosages.

Find a vet experienced in treating toy breeds.

You are ultimately responsible for your dog's health care. To make effective decisions, you must feel comfortable communicating with your vet. You may need to ask questions about treatment options, drug interactions, or side effects, or you may need to ask for estimates for various procedures. The vet should be willing to do some research if your questions can't be answered right away. If she seems dismissive or disinterested about your concerns, find someone else.

A personal recommendation is the easiest way to find a good vet for your Maltese. If you acquired your dog from a local breeder, she may ask you to use a particular vet. Otherwise, try contacting dog clubs in your area to find vets whom toy breeders recommend. Or you can prepare a list of questions and conduct your own search.

What to Look For

If you've found a vet who you think might be right for your Maltese, visit the clinic and ask these questions:

- Does the clinic belong to a certification program, such as the American Animal Hospital Association (AAHA)? (www.aahanet.org)
- Does it offer special services, like house calls, grooming, boarding, or emergency care?
- Are hospitalized pets monitored overnight?
- Does it offer any specialties, like orthopedics or acupuncture?
- If you are interested in alternative medicine, does the vet offer this

FAMILY-FRIENDLY TIP

Visiting the Vet

From a child's point of view, the vet's office is a fascinating place. It's natural for a child to be curious and excited. Make sure that your child understands that many of the pets there are not feeling well. They need to be quiet and may not appreciate being petted. There is also a possibility of spreading infection if a child does not wash her hands thoroughly after touching sick pets in a vet's waiting room. If your Maltese is somewhat nervous visiting the vet, ask your child to help to keep him calm by petting and talking to him throughout the visit.

specialty, or is she willing to provide referrals?
- How do the fees for typical services, such as office visits, vaccinations, or neutering, compare with other clinics?
- What payment options does the clinic accept?
- If you have health insurance for your Maltese, does it accept your insurance plan?

If you like what you hear, take your dog for a routine exam. Check out the

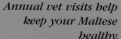
Annual vet visits help keep your Maltese healthy.

clinic and the vet while she checks out your dog.

- Is the clinic clean and inviting?
- Do the staff members relate well to the animals?
- Are the staff members pleasant and professional to the clients?

During the exam, pay attention to the vet's demeanor and technique. She should be thorough, reassuring, and genuinely interested in your dog's care. The vet should not try to intimidate you or talk you into unnecessary tests or treatments.

Annual Vet Visit

Schedule a routine checkup for your Maltese within two or three days of getting him. This will confirm that he is in good health at the time of sale or possibly identify a pre-existing health problem that the breeder was not aware of. After that, you probably won't need to go back to the vet until his next annual checkup.

Owners usually schedule an annual vet visit when their dog is due for booster vaccinations. While recently updated vaccination protocols have shown that yearly boosters may not be necessary, there are several other important reasons to go. Your Maltese should be checked for intestinal parasites every year. They don't always cause obvious symptoms, but these will become worse if untreated. Heartworm has become prevalent in much of the US, but year-round protection isn't always needed. Because it's spread by mosquitoes, climate and location will be the deciding factors. Your dog will need a blood test before starting on a preventive.

During a general health exam, your vet will ask if your dog has been eating, drinking, and eliminating normally. She will make sure that the dog's heart and respiration rates are normal and check his weight, body temperature, joint mobility, general responsiveness, and skin and coat condition. She will also examine his ears, throat, mouth, gums, and teeth for signs of infection, as well as perform a routine eye exam.

This is the time to mention any concerns about your pet's health. Your vet may reassure you that it's nothing to worry about, or it may be an early symptom of a problem that should be brought to the vet's attention.

Vaccinations

Puppies receive their first immunity from their mother's milk within a few hours of birth. This protects them for

Neutering

Unless you plan to breed or show your Maltese, have him neutered. Most breeders insist on this when placing their pet-quality puppies. Neutering ensures that only the best dogs contribute to the next generation's gene pool. More importantly, it prevents the possibility of unwanted puppies resulting from accidental or irresponsible breeding.

Neutering is a safe, routine procedure for both sexes, but it is major surgery. Your breeder may advise waiting until a puppy reaches a certain age or weight before having him neutered to minimize risks. In addition to preventing problems associated with twice yearly heat cycles, neutered females have no risk of developing reproductive-related disorders, and they have a much lower risk of mammary cancer if neutered before their third heat or before they reach two-and-a-half years of age. Males neutered before puberty, which takes place at about six to nine months of age, never develop some typical male behaviors, such as territorial leg lifting.

Neutering can prevent or minimize many undesirable habits, but it is not an instant cure for chronic bad behaviors, like house soiling or mounting. In these cases, neutering must be combined with behavior modification.

If possible, schedule other necessary surgical procedures at the same time, such as umbilical hernia repair or extraction of retained puppy teeth. Many vets also recommend microchip implantation if the dog is already anesthetized for some other reason.

Maltese

optimum protection and minimal risk.

Vaccinations will not be effective until a puppy's maternal immunity has worn off, and this is subject to individual variation. For small breeds like Maltese, some vets and breeders recommend waiting until a puppy is at least eight weeks old to maximize effectiveness and minimize risk. Puppy vaccinations should be administered at least three weeks apart to ensure the best immune response. The first vaccination doesn't always produce complete immunity and must be repeated with two to three booster shots. Occasionally, immunity doesn't occur until the third vaccination. Keep your puppy away from places frequented by other dogs until he's completed all his puppy shots.

about 6 to 12 weeks. After that, they need a series of vaccinations to protect them from many potentially lethal canine diseases.

In recent years, dog owners have become more concerned about the safety and effectiveness of vaccines. It's true that excessive vaccinations can be harmful, but contagious diseases like distemper pose a greater risk. New vaccine technology and revised recommendations provide

Your vet and breeder can recommend the best vaccination schedule for your Maltese.

Combination Vaccinations

Vaccinations are usually administered as one combined shot, known as the DHLPP (distemper, hepatitis (adenovirus), leptospirosis, parainfluenza, parvovirus) vaccination. Some combination vaccines contain as many as seven components, and your Maltese may not need all of these. Ask your vet exactly what's in a combination vaccination, and inquire about the potential risks of each ingredient.

Dogs in rural areas or who have regular contact with other dogs at grooming shops or kennels need enhanced protection. Regardless of age or location, all dogs should be vaccinated against distemper, parvovirus, adenovirus, and rabies. These diseases are highly contagious and usually fatal, and they remain prevalent throughout the country. Rabies vaccination is mandatory in every state.

Rabies vaccination should always be given separately from the DHLPP shot, and most breeders prefer not to give any rabies shots to Maltese puppies under six months of age.

- **Distemper** is a highly contagious viral disease, the most dreaded canine killer until recent decades. It is rarely seen today but is still present in all dog populations, transmitted by direct contact with droplets from infected dogs. Symptoms include depression, loss of appetite, vomiting, diarrhea, nasal and ocular discharge, seizures, and paralysis. Bronchitis and pneumonia are

common complications.

- **Canine parvovirus** is a highly contagious viral infection transmitted by contact with infected fecal matter. It is easily spread to dogs on human shoes or clothing. Dogs of all ages are susceptible, but puppies are at the greatest risk. The virus attacks the gastrointestinal system, causing sudden severe vomiting, bloody diarrhea, dehydration, and shock.

- **Infectious canine hepatitis** is a highly contagious viral disease spread by direct or indirect contact from the urine and feces of infected dogs. Symptoms include

The Expert Knows

Vaccine Reactions

Reactions to routine vaccinations are rare, but they are more common in toy breeds like Maltese. They can occur immediately or days or weeks later. A reaction may be characterized by lethargy, loss of appetite, mild fever, and muscle soreness that resolve within a day or two. Severe allergic reactions can include hives, facial swelling, shock, and seizures. Sensitivities to vaccines can be hereditary, and your breeder can tell you if your dog has a potential risk for reacting to a particular type of vaccine and recommend the safest vaccination routine. Many Maltese breeders prefer not to administer the leptospirosis vaccine, because it has caused anaphylactic reactions in the breed. Today, most combination vaccines can be found without the lepto vaccine.

conjunctivitis, tonsillitis, loss of appetite, jaundice, and abdominal tenderness caused by gall bladder and liver inflammation. Recovered animals can become carriers, harboring the virus in their kidneys and spreading infection through their urine.

- **Rabies** is a viral infection that attacks the central nervous system. All warm-blooded species are susceptible. It is carried and spread through the saliva of infected individuals. Symptoms include disorientation, headache, fretfulness, drooling, seizures, and hallucinations. Once symptoms appear, rabies is always fatal.

- **Leptospirosis** bacteria attack the pancreas, liver, and kidneys. It is spread by animals such as rats, raccoons, skunks, and possums or through contact with infected soil or vegetation. Bacteria can survive for months in standing water. Although leptospirosis is usually associated with rural environments, urban dogs can be at the greatest risk. It is transmissible from dogs to humans through contact with infected urine. Symptoms include fever, muscle pain, lack of appetite, extreme thirst, and leg swelling. Prognosis for recovery is poor, and

Maltese

Some vaccinations are recommended based on the area in which you live.

infection can lead to liver or kidney failure.

- **Kennel cough** is a highly contagious airborne disease caused by bacteria, a virus, or combinations of infectious agents. The resulting upper airway inflammation is rarely fatal to adult dogs but can cause serious infection or pneumonia in puppies. This disease is characterized by a constant hacking cough, and touching an affected dog's throat is usually enough to trigger a coughing attack. Stressful, crowded kennels, pet shops, and animal shelters are common sources of infection. Dogs at high risk should be revaccinated twice yearly. Nasal vaccines are considered safer and more reliable.

- **Canine Lyme disease** is spread by deer ticks. Unlike human victims, infected dogs do not exhibit the telltale "bull's eye" rash. Typical symptoms include limping, joint pain, fever, loss of appetite, and swollen lymph nodes. If you suspect that your Maltese has been infected, speedy diagnosis and treatment are crucial. Ticks

First Aid

Rule one of first aid is *don't panic*. Most pets will suffer some kind of health emergency during their lifetime. Your dog's life may depend on your ability to calmly assess the situation and respond quickly and appropriately. Otherwise, you may overreact to a minor health issue or underestimate the seriousness of a life-threatening condition.

Keep a kit of first-aid supplies, fully stocked and updated. It should include a comprehensive first-aid handbook, the phone number of the animal poison control center (1-888-426-4435—there is a charge per call), and driving directions to your nearest 24-hour emergency vet clinic.

First-aid supplies to keep on hand include gauze, bandages, and first-aid tape; temporary splinting materials such as a large plastic spoon or paint stick; oral glucose solution and dosing syringe; over-the-counter medications to control vomiting and diarrhea; clotting powder to stop minor bleeding; peroxide or disinfectant solution to clean wounds; Benadryl to counteract allergic reactions; buffered baby aspirin; cortisone ointment for minor skin irritations; artificial tears or sterile eye wash; thermometer; tweezers; pen light; and blunt-tipped scissors.

A pet emergency first-aid course can help to prepare you to evaluate and handle emergencies, including basic demonstrations in administering mouth to snout resuscitation and CPR. These courses are available through your local Red Cross.

Feeling Good

should be carefully removed with tweezers, placed in a sealed container, and analyzed by your vet. If you live in a high-risk area, your vet may recommend vaccinating your Maltese against Lyme disease.

When to Vaccinate

The newest AAHA guidelines recommend that a puppy's initial DHLPP vaccination series be repeated one year later and again every three years thereafter.

The duration of immunity provided by different vaccinations can vary from a few months to seven years. You can ask your vet to test your dog's antibody titer level to determine when booster shots are needed.

After your dog is vaccinated, his immunity to disease occurs gradually, depending on many factors. Among other things, human studies have shown that stress influences the number of antibodies produced in response to vaccines. If possible, then, vaccinations should not be scheduled right before a potentially stressful event, such as being boarded at a kennel.

Breed-Specific Illnesses

In addition to the general illnesses that can afflict any dog, every breed is prone to some special problems. This doesn't mean that every Maltese is at risk for these ailments, though. Responsible breeders do their best to ensure that this is not the case. However, a higher than normal

Good breeders work to reduce inherited diseases in their dogs.

incidence of the following disorders has been documented in the breed.

Hepatic Portosystemic Shunt

Hepatic portosystemic shunt, also known as liver shunt, is a congenital disorder causing the body's blood supply to bypass the liver, where harmful toxins are normally filtered out. Symptoms vary, depending on the severity of the defect. Stunted growth, failure to gain weight, and poor appetite are often the earliest signs. Other symptoms include weakness,

vomiting, diarrhea, seizures, and drooling. A definitive diagnosis is made through a combination of blood tests, X-rays, and an ultrasound. Corrective surgery is the recommended treatment.

Patellar Luxation

Patellar luxation is comparable to dislocation of the kneecap. Most prevalent in toy breeds, it has also been documented in larger breeds, mixed breeds, and cats. Your veterinarian can identify the condition without x-ray evaluation. Mildly affected dogs may not exhibit pain or limping. Severe cases can lead to lameness or degenerative joint disease. Mild cases may not require any treatment other than controlled exercise to minimize stress on the weakened joint. Severe cases may benefit from orthopedic surgery to repair the damaged joint.

Patent Ductus Arteriosus

Patent ductus arteriosus (PDA) causes abnormal blood flow and is the most common congenital heart defect in dogs. It is documented in many breeds and is more common in females. The severity of the defect varies, ranging from no visible symptoms to coughing, weakness, and labored breathing. The characteristic heart murmur can be diagnosed soon after birth and confirmed with an electrocardiogram and X-rays. Depending on the type and severity of the malformation, PDA may be treated with medications or surgically corrected when a puppy is two to four months old.

White Shaker Dog Syndrome

Also known as idiopathic tremor syndrome, this neurological disorder affects several breeds of small white dogs. Typical symptoms of tremors, head tilt, difficulty walking, and uncoordinated eye movements develop suddenly in dogs aged six months to three years. Most dogs respond well to medication and show

Giving Pills

The easiest way to trick your dog into taking a pill is to hide it in a treat. Use something irresistibly tasty and easily rolled into a ball, like cream cheese or liverwurst. The treat must be small enough to be "gulped" without chewing but with no danger of choking.

If that doesn't work, gently open your dog's mouth by pressing his lips over his molars. Place the pill as far back on his tongue as possible, and hold the mouth shut. Once the pill is in position, distract him by blowing on his nose, stroking his neck, and talking to him until he swallows.

Internal Parasites

Internal parasites include protozoal and worm infestations.

Coccidia and Giardia

Coccidia and giardia are protozoal infections transmitted through fecal matter in contaminated soil, food, or most commonly, water. Symptoms include periodic bouts of watery diarrhea, poor appetite, weight loss, and dehydration. Illness is often triggered by stress. Both of these intestinal diseases can be transmitted from dogs to humans. Diagnosis can be tricky, because protozoa are not detectable in every fecal sample from an infected dog.

62

improvement within a few days. Some dogs will require lifelong medication to control symptoms.

Parasites and Other Problems

Parasites can afflict any dog. Don't assume that your Maltese is not at risk because he is a house dog or because he spends very little time around other dogs. In adult dogs, early symptoms may not be obvious, which is why every dog should be checked for parasites annually. If neglected, they will eventually undermine his general health.

Heartworm

Heartworm is exactly what it sounds like: worms lodged in your dog's heart. The infection begins when a mosquito carrying heartworm larvae bites your dog. The larvae travel through the bloodstream to the heart, where they can grow 14 inches long. Over

Food and environmental allergies are the most common types.

Maltese

Allergies

Allergies cause the immune system to react against something that it normally considers to be harmless, like pollen or plastic. Allergens can enter your dog's system in several ways, like through food and the environment.

Food and environmental allergies are the most common types. Environmental allergies often have a familial link, and older dogs can be more prone to develop allergies due to lowered immune function.

Most common symptoms of allergies include persistent licking and scratching. Untreated, or treated unsuccessfully, minor skin irritation can become a secondary bacterial or fungal infection. Your vet will do a series of skin tests to discover the substance that is causing your dog's allergy. Once identified, hyposensitization, vaccinating to stimulate immunity to the allergic substance, often alleviates symptoms for many dogs.

time, they will impair heart function. Heartworm can be treated, but the treatment is dangerous and sometimes fatal. If you live in an area where heartworm is prevalent, put your dog on a preventive. New medications can be given monthly or even biannually and many also protect against intestinal parasites.

Roundworms, Hookworms, and Tapeworms

Checking for roundworms, hookworms, and tapeworms should be part of your dog's annual checkup. The most common symptoms are lethargy, diarrhea, vomiting, failure to gain weight, and a pot-bellied appearance. Severe cases can lead to anemia and respiratory complications. All puppies should be checked for hookworms and roundworms because they can acquire them from their dam during pregnancy or nursing. Both roundworms and hookworms can be transmitted to humans, so always wash your hands after handling or petting dogs with whom you are not familiar.

Tapeworms are carried by fleas harboring tapeworm eggs and are transmitted to dogs when they accidentally ingest a flea. If your dog has a problem with fleas, he should be checked for tapeworms. Typical symptoms include occasional vomiting, diarrhea, and noticeable weight loss. Tapeworm segments, shed in feces, look like grains of rice.

Your vet will prescribe an appropriate dewormer, which may need to be administered several times to break the life cycle of the parasite. Deworming will not solve the problem unless you discover the source of the infestation and prevent recurrence.

This can range from contaminated soil or water to contact with infected wild or stray animals.

External Parasites

External parasites include fleas, mites, and ticks.

Fleas

Dogs most often catch fleas from cats or by visiting areas frequented by cats. The first sign of the problem is usually persistent scratching. Fleas and gritty black flea dirt are easy to spot on thinly coated areas like your dog's tummy.

There are many flea-control products on the market, ranging from dips, powders, and baths to oral and topical preventives. Ask your vet or breeder to recommend the safest, most effective one for your Maltese, and never use multiple products. Flea control must include treating the environment to get rid of fleas and eggs on bedding, furniture, rugs, and lawns.

Mites

Several species of microscopic mites cause mange, with the most common type being demodectic mange. Many dogs carry demodex mites without developing symptoms. Puppies and older dogs are most susceptible because their natural resistance is lower. Symptoms include itching, flaky skin, hair loss, and crusty areas on the muzzle, face, and ears.

A less common form is sarcoptic mange, known as scabies, which causes intense itching and oozing skin sores. Cheyletiella mange, known as "walking dandruff," is most common in puppies. This is the least serious form of mange and causes mild itching and skin flaking on the head, neck, and back.

Mange is diagnosed by microscopic examination of skin scrapings. It is contagious, so if you have other pets, it's a good idea to have them checked, even if they don't show symptoms. Treatment consists of medicated dips or baths done under veterinary supervision. The dog's bedding and grooming equipment should be disinfected or replaced as well.

Ticks

Ticks are easy to spot on Maltese, and they are most often found on the ears, face, head, or feet. They hop a ride on your dog when he brushes against them on leaves or grass. You can reduce the risk by applying tick repellant. (Never use multiple flea- and tick-control products on your dog. Every flea- and tick-control product is potentially toxic, and mixing products can increase this toxicity or enhance the risk of drug interactions.)

To remove a tick, grasp it as close to the skin as possible with a hemostat or tweezers, and pull it off. Don't try to burn it off or apply gasoline or kerosene to your dog's skin. Crush or burn the tick immediately after removal.

If your Maltese seems ill after being bitten by a tick or traveling to a tick-infested area, have him tested for ehrlichiosis, Rocky Mountain spotted fever, babesiosis, tick paralysis, and Lyme disease.

Ringworm

Contrary to its name, ringworm has nothing to do with worms. It's a fungal infection that causes small, round, scaly bald spots and intense itching. Ringworm is transmissible between dogs and from dogs to humans. Treatment can take up to two months and includes oral and topical medications combined with scrupulous cleaning to get rid of any fungus spores on rugs, furniture, or bedding.

Hot Spots and Flea Bite Allergy

Red, irritated bald patches can be caused by allergies, mats, or fleabites. Licking and scratching the irritation make it worse and can cause secondary bacterial infections. Maltese can be allergic to the proteins in flea saliva that are injected into a dog's bloodstream as the fleas feed.

You may want to explore alternate therapies for your Maltese.

Known as flea allergy dermatitis, this can be a much bigger problem than the fleas.

Your vet will prescribe a combination of topical and oral antibiotics, as well as cortisone to control itching and inflammation. The inflamed area should be cleaned and treated with antiseptics, and the hair must be clipped away. Keep your dog's nails trimmed short, and try to prevent him from biting and scratching the area.

Alternative Therapies

Complementary and alternative medicine (CAM) has recently gained much wider acceptance in the veterinary community. It's not unusual to find vets offering both conventional and alternative treatments or suggesting alternative therapies when standard treatments fail. They can be especially valuable for toy breeds susceptible to drug reactions and side effects from standard treatments.

Alternative medicine includes a broad array of therapies, such as herbal medicine, homeopathy, and acupuncture. When choosing one for your Maltese, safety *and* effectiveness should be your priorities. Some alternative therapies have been subjected to thorough research and clinical trials, but not all. Many areas of veterinary alternative medicine are poorly regulated because they don't fall under any legal definition of veterinary care. Gather as much information as you

can before making a decision. If your research turns up nothing but glowing personal testimonials, be skeptical.

Many CAM specialties have licensing and certification programs. If an alternative practitioner is not a licensed veterinarian, check her qualifications. Human practitioners may be quite knowledgeable in their field, but this doesn't guarantee expertise in treating animals.

The practitioner should frankly discuss the number of treatments, the potential time frame, and estimated costs of treatment. Beware of anyone making outlandish claims or vague promises about what they can do for your pet.

Monitor your dog closely during treatment for signs of relapse or bad reactions. The fact that a medication is made from natural ingredients does not guarantee complete safety. Side effects, overdosing, and drug interactions are all possible. If your dog's condition worsens or does not respond to the treatment within a reasonable amount of time, don't hesitate to seek another opinion.

Maltese

SENIOR DOG TIP
Senior Dog Health

As your Maltese ages, you may need to revise certain aspects of his care to meet his changing needs. Older dogs don't adapt well to changes in their environment or routine. Your vet can test your Maltese for hearing or vision loss, which may be the underlying reason for inattentiveness or disorientation. Try to ensure that he sticks to his routine, including getting some exercise every day, even if it's just a short walk to the corner. Older dogs need to relieve themselves more often, and your pet may need more frequent potty breaks to prevent housetraining lapses. If your senior Maltese begins to have housetraining lapses, your vet can help you to pinpoint the cause.

Older Maltese can develop dental problems despite dedicated cleaning. Tooth decay can cause a painful dental abscess or spread to become a life-threatening systemic infection. This may be the underlying reason for listlessness, irritability, or poor appetite. A dog gradually feels less hungry as he becomes accustomed to not eating. You will need to stimulate his appetite to break this cycle.

Older pets deserve to be indulged, but don't let yours become overweight. Older dogs are less active, and excess weight can intensify pre-existing health problems, especially degenerative joint disease. Lack of energy or a reluctance to exercise can be due to age-related muscle or joint pain. If you suspect that your Maltese is suffering from arthritis, your vet will prescribe appropriate anti-inflammatory pain relievers. Older dogs also might appreciate a heating pad or orthopedic dog bed to ease joint and muscle stiffness.

Senior dogs should receive semi-annual vet checks. Caught early, some age-related health issues can be effectively managed; others can be entirely prevented. Your vet may recommend blood tests, X-rays, or a urinalysis as part of a senior dog's regular health exam.

Unusual problems such as sudden weight loss, pain, labored breathing, difficulty moving or urinating, and refusal to eat merit an immediate vet exam. Senior dogs are more susceptible to common illnesses, and minor ailments can quickly turn serious.

If your dog takes daily prescription drugs, check with your vet to ensure that there is no danger of a drug interaction before giving over-the-counter medications. Some over-the-counter drugs should never be given to pets with pre-existing health disorders.

Chapter 6

Being Good

Our society has become increasingly intolerant of unruly dogs, and every dog lover has a responsibility to ensure that her pet does not provide justification for this stance. A well-trained dog is not only an object of admiration; your dog's good behavior enhances your quality of life. Many owners make the mistake of thinking that discipline will undermine their dog's trust and affection. Dogs are pack animals, socially attuned to understanding pack rules. They want to follow your rules and fit in with your pack. If anything, fair, consistent leadership serves to enhance the human/canine bond.

Socialization

Dogs employ the same social skills to interact with humans and other dogs. Puppies start learning these from their dam when they are three weeks old. By six weeks, they begin socializing with their littermates, their breeder, and all the pets and people in that household. This is a good introduction, but it's just the beginning. Puppies must practice these skills every day to become well-socialized adults. This will come easily for confident puppies, but even introverts will become socially skilled given enough encouragement and practice.

A puppy's natural socialization period ends around 14 weeks of age. Although he must be protected from disease risks until he is completely vaccinated, don't put off socialization. Instead, take him out in a dog carrier or pet stroller, take him for a ride in the car, or visit places that are not frequented by other dogs.

While consistent socialization has a cumulative effect, it turns out that dogs don't generalize very well. Puppies need exposure to many different people, places, and pets. A puppy may be perfectly at ease with familiar individuals but become apprehensive when meeting someone who looks or acts differently. For instance, if a puppy has been socialized to only adults, he'll need extra time to get used to children, cats, and other types of animals.

Even well-socialized puppies can become wary of familiar people or places during stages of fear and shyness that often accompany adolescence. This is why it's so important to continue socialization until adulthood.

If your puppy acts shy when introduced to new people and places, arrange short, welcoming "get acquainted" visits. Doing so will calm his fears and

Maltese

Puppies need exposure to many different people, places, and pets.

minimize the possibility that he will develop a phobia during an actual vet exam or grooming appointment.

Children

Small dogs who haven't been raised around children can find them intimidating. Children tend to move faster and speak louder than adults, which can seem threatening to a tiny dog. Give your dog time to get used to a child's manner, and make sure that the child approaches the dog calmly and gently. It's probably safest to have both of them sit on the floor when first meeting. Show the child how to interact with the dog without frightening him. Never permit a child to grab, chase, or corner a dog. If the dog is too heavy for a child or fears being picked up, don't try it.

A successful relationship between a child and a small dog doesn't happen overnight. It requires socialization, education, and constant supervision. A child may not realize that some games are too rough or frightening for a small dog. Play sessions between puppies and children are a major source of potential problems because everyone tends to get a little out of control. Children should be taught to respect the dog's need to retreat and understand that he is off-limits when resting.

Cats and Other Animals

All interactions must be supervised when first introducing your Maltese to other animals. Maltese are generally friendly toward other pets, but there

FAMILY-FRIENDLY TIP

Children and Training

A child's involvement can either reinforce or undermine a dog's training. Participation in the training process helps them to understand how it's done and why it is so important. Children less than six years old may be too young to work with the dog but can always dole out treats and praise for a job well done. They should not encourage bad habits like jumping or barking, even if they are too young to do the training.

Junior dog-training classes are a great way to simultaneously train your Maltese and familiarize your child with appropriate, safe ways to interact and communicate with dogs.

71

Being Good

is no guarantee that this attitude will be mutual. Some species are naturally fearful or defensive toward dogs, and separation may be the safest course. Keep your Maltese away from other pets' food, bedding, or droppings. Allowing him to have access to these things can trigger disagreements over territory or lead to illness from the ingestion of things like kitty litter or birdseed.

If your Maltese is not used to cats, your introduction strategy will depend on the cat's temperament. In general, dogs are more sociable than cats. Some cats are naturally shy and prefer to retreat, rather than interact with, a dog. Trying to force a friendship will only make things worse—and never underestimate the damage that a small cat can inflict on a small dog.

If the cat seems okay around the dog, keep the dog restrained for the first meeting. Watch the cat's expressions and body language for signs of fear or aggression. And remember that dogs and cats speak different languages. For instance, rolling over is a friendly, playful gesture from a dog's point of view, but a cat might perceive it as an intention to fight. As long as both of them seem calm and interested, let them get acquainted. But make sure that the cat always has an escape route if he becomes frightened.

With daily, supervised visits, it may take anywhere from a week, a month, or even longer for your pets to accept each other. During this time, the cat must always have complete access to his regular territory.

Other Dogs

The relative size and age of each dog is a primary consideration when introducing a Maltese into your canine pack. Maltese are typically friendly, but as breeder Vicki Fierheller points out, "It is too easy for a large dog to inadvertently hurt a toy puppy." You must have a way to keep them separated when they cannot be supervised until you are certain that they are getting along together.

Dogs use face and body gestures to show their mood and intentions, which help to predict their behavior

Supervise dog introductions until you know that they are getting along.

during encounters. You must pay attention and correctly interpret these signals. The fact that they are getting along fine one minute doesn't mean that that can't change.

At first, keep both dogs on lead or separated by a barrier. If they seem friendly, allow them to get close and sniff each other. End the visit if either one shows indications of aggression or fear. Most dogs are interested in socializing, and a friendship will develop between them in time. Human interventions to speed things up, like reallocating food or toys, can make matters worse by encouraging rivalries and dominance problems. Insisting on instant friendship between hesitant dogs can permanently undermine this possibility.

Crate Training

A crate satisfies a dog's basic territorial instincts, which should simplify crate training and create a positive association, as long as you don't undermine it. Never use the crate for punishment or as a handy way to put your dog in "storage." The crate should be used to keep your Maltese out of harm's way. This may include times when you cannot adequately supervise him or when gardeners or workers are in your home and might inadvertently

The Expert Knows

Communication

Dog training is a two-way street. You must communicate clearly and understand your dog's responses. Always use the proper voice tone, facial expression, and body language to reinforce your message—like using a neutral voice when giving commands, using a softer, higher tone for praise, and using a low, clipped tone for corrections. Combining vocal commands with hand signals emphasizes your message and holds your dog's attention. Always give vocal and visual cues simultaneously, and use exactly the same ones for a specific command.

Your dog cannot learn unless he's paying attention. He should appear calm and alert, looking directly at you with his tail moving in a low, relaxed wag. If he's confused or nervous, his head will be lowered, his ears will be folded back, he won't make eye contact, and he may shake, whine, yawn, or sniff and paw the ground.

73

leave a gate or door open. It is also an excellent way to keep him safe during car travel or trips to the vet or groomer.

Devise a crate-training schedule appropriate to your dog's age. Sticking to the schedule ensures that your dog knows when he is expected to go in his crate and when he will be coming out. Young puppies should only be crated for two hours at most. Feeding a puppy in the crate encourages a good attitude, but crate him before—not after—feeding, because he will need to eliminate soon after eating.

Crate time can be increased by one to two hours per month. A twelve-week-old puppy should be able to spend three or four hours crated. By five months of age he should be able to make it through the night confined to the crate. Puppies usually learn to control the urge to eliminate during the night by the time they are six or eight weeks old, but sometimes they will have to get up for this during the night. Keep the crate near your bed and be prepared to get up and take your dog out. Otherwise, he may start going to the bathroom in his crate. Once this habit becomes established, it is very difficult to discourage.

Never force your Maltese into the crate. Ask him to go in using a special command, and reward him when he does. Hiding a treat in the back of the crate helps. When you want him to come out, open the door, give the command, and reward him when he does. Never encourage him to jump out or whine in anticipation of getting out.

Many puppies protest by digging, whining, or barking when crate training begins. This is normal and usually stops pretty quickly. Put a comfortable bed and a few toys in the crate. Don't leave water in there during training unless you want to clean up the mess. Your puppy will soon fall asleep or occupy himself with a toy when he realizes that his antics aren't getting any reaction from you.

Housetraining

Housetraining basically reinforces a dog's natural instinct to keep his

Crates are useful when traveling with your Maltese.

environment clean. As soon as they can walk, puppies try to eliminate away from areas where they eat or sleep. Reinforcing this behavior is far easier than revising bad habits later.

Toy breeds have a reputation for being hard to housetrain. In reality, housetraining a small dog is not difficult. In some ways, it may be easier than housetraining a bigger dog. Owners usually keep a much closer eye on what a small dog is up to, and toy breeds like Maltese have a strong motivation to please. They will happily do what you ask as long as they understand the rules.

Consistency Is Key

Regardless of whether you are housetraining a puppy or an adult, the same rules apply: consistency, vigilance, and positive reinforcement. If you bring home a new Maltese who is already housetrained, this will ensure that he makes the transition without a housetraining lapse.

You must restrict your dog's territory during housetraining. Don't complicate matters by expecting him to search for the right spot when he needs to go. This also makes it impossible to supervise his activities. Vigilant supervision is so important for housetraining toy breeds because accidents can go unnoticed until much later. A dog can form a habit of eliminating in an unwanted spot before you even notice what he's up to. If this occurs, you must begin the whole process all over again.

A dog's instinct to keep his territory clean doesn't apply to places outside his immediate eating and sleeping area. In these other cases, his impulse is quite the opposite. Elimination becomes a handy way to mark territory unless you provide a more rewarding alternative.

You must consistently take your dog to the proper location, be it a litterbox, newspaper, or the lamppost down the street. Accompany him every time to make sure that he actually does what he is there for—and to praise him when he does. Try using a specific command for this, such as "Go potty." Positive feedback, praise, and treats must be immediate.

Give him plenty of time to go, at least 15 to 20 minutes, and don't distract him from his mission. If he doesn't go within that time, don't assume that he really didn't need to, a common housetraining error. Crate him for an hour, and take him back to the spot until you get the desired results. This can be time consuming, a reason why many owners don't do a good job of it.

Your dog's elimination schedule is directly linked to his feeding schedule, so sticking to his routine is crucial. Adult Maltese should be taken out first thing in the morning, once in the afternoon, in the early evening, and before bed. Young puppies may need to urinate every one to two hours and defecate four or five times a day. Maturity, not training, is the only thing that will speed up bladder and bowel control, so don't expect too much from a puppy. They are going to have accidents.

Consistency is key when housetraining your Maltese.

Finding a Trainer

Dog trainers are not equally skilled in working with toy breeds, and Maltese don't respond equally well to all training methods. The training environment is just as important, as are the trainer's skills and approach. Avoid trainers who utilize harsh methods or teach crowded classes that contain large or unruly dogs.

Before choosing a trainer, sit in on a class. Observe the trainer's methods, demeanor, and ability to control the class. Every dog and handler should receive some personal attention. The trainer should put dogs and handlers at ease and encourage their confidence. Visit the Association of Pet Dog Trainers' website for tips on finding a trainer at www.apdt.com.

Puppies can't be expected to let you know when they need to go, but once you are familiar with your dog's habits, this becomes easy to predict. Learn to spot behavior cues that indicate that he needs to go, like scratching at the door, circling, whining, and sniffing.

Accidents Happen

If you catch your Maltese in the act of having an accident, firmly tell him "No," and take him to his appropriate spot. Don't punish him or frighten him—this is a sensitive breed. Reprimanding a Maltese after a housetraining accident is pointless. Dogs are not good at making appropriate connections between past behavior and your displeasure, but they will understand that you are very upset about something.

Accidents must be cleaned up thoroughly to remove any traces of odor. Dogs can smell minute concentrations of urine that we would never notice. The lingering odor will lure him back to the spot to eliminate there again, and if you have other pets, they may also begin doing the same thing.

A few successful experiences means that your message is getting across; it doesn't mean that a reliable habit has

Don't punish your Maltese for housetraining mistakes.

been established. That takes time and repetition, and some dogs need more than others.

If your housetraining routine doesn't yield immediate results, switching methods will only confuse your dog and prolong the process. Settle on one housetraining strategy before you bring your Maltese home. Begin as soon as he arrives, and stick to it even if immediate results do not live up to your expectations.

Dogs can be trained to vary their elimination habits, such as using a litterbox indoors and going for a walk or using a doggy door to go out in the yard. If you want to use one of these methods, it's important to introduce your dog to varied elimination routines and surfaces by four months of age. It's more difficult for a dog to revise established habits after that age.

Basic Commands

It's easiest to train a dog to do something on command that comes naturally to him. Simply get in the habit of giving the appropriate command when your dog sits, lies down, or comes to you. Especially for puppies, short 5- to 15-minute frequent training sessions are more effective than lengthy repetitive drilling. Keep distractions to a minimum, and end every session on a positive note.

Come

This is the first and most important command to teach your dog. Coming immediately when called can literally save your dog's life. You never know when he might slip his lead or escape from your yard. A wild or panicked dog can easily outrun any human and may just keep going under these circumstances.

Practice this command a lot, even after you're sure that your dog knows it. Puppies will come to you instinctively, and most of your work involves reinforcing this natural inclination.

When teaching the *come* command, first set your dog up for success by giving the command when he's already

Treats for Training

Irresistible treats are the best way to reinforce training. Training treats should be something extra tasty and easily chewed. Pieces should be no bigger than your pinkie nail. Bits of cheese, chopped up hot dog, steak, chicken, apple or carrot, plain popcorn, Cheerios, or tiny canine training treats all work fine. Some dogs have a favorite, which should be reserved strictly for training. Mixing them up can make training even more interesting for your dog.

heading toward you. Get down to your dog's eye level, say "Come," and lure him with a treat or toy. When he begins to approach, pour on the praise. If he stops halfway, keep up the encouragement until he comes up to you for his reward. If he responds slowly or goes the other way, never lose your temper, drag him toward you, or chase him. Ignoring a dog or walking away is often enough to prompt him to follow you. As soon as he does, repeat the command and follow up with praise and a reward.

Sit

Teaching your Maltese to sit on command is more than a parlor trick or dog show exercise—it can make your life a lot easier. Guests may not always appreciate a rousing Maltese welcome, and you may enjoy eating your dinner in peace. These are perfect situations when the *sit* comes in very handy.

To teach this command, sit or kneel in front of your Maltese, holding a treat in front of his nose. Slowly raise the treat over his head. As his head goes up to follow your hand, the other end

will probably go down. As his rump starts to descend, say "Sit," giving the treat and plenty of praise as soon as he does. Once your dog has mastered the *sit*, he's on his way to learning *stay* and *down*.

Stay

Like *come* and *sit*, this command can be useful in your daily routine. For

Maltese

Use small treats for training your dog.

instance, *stay* can be handy when teaching your Maltese to stand still for bathing or brushing. Even little things like attaching a lead become far easier with a stationary dog. This command takes some practice, especially for puppies with short attention spans.

To teach this command, tell your dog to sit, and follow up by saying "Stay." (It helps to combine the command with a hand signal, such as a "traffic cop" gesture with arm outstretched and palm open.) Take a few steps back, repeating the command and hand signal. If your dog gets up, return him to the spot and repeat the command. After he stays in place for a few seconds, tell him to come, and reward him with treats and praise. Gradually increase the time of the *stay* and the distance between you and your dog.

The sit command can be useful when guests come to the door.

Down
Because it is a more relaxed position, the *down* can be used instead of the *sit* at times when you want your Maltese to stay in one place for any length of time.

To teach *down*, tell your dog to sit and kneel down in front of him, holding a treat in front of his nose. As you lower the treat, his head and body should follow. Praise him as soon as he starts to comply, and give him a treat when he does. This may take a few tries, so be patient and encouraging. Don't force him into a *down* position by pressing on his back or shoulders; dogs usually react by pushing in the opposite direction.

Walk Nicely (Heel)
Even a tiny Maltese should learn to walk calmly at your side on lead. This is mandatory if you plan to show him in conformation or obedience, but that's not the only reason. A wildly lunging dog is a nuisance to fellow dog walkers and pedestrians, and a toy dog can put itself into serious danger with these antics. Puppies

should be introduced to a light buckle collar at eight weeks. Within another week, begin attaching the lead and encouraging him to follow you. Some puppies do this right away, while others need a few weeks. Never jerk on the lead or pull the puppy along. Your goal is to teach him to walk when you say "Heel" while maintaining your pace on a loose lead.

Traditionally, dogs are taught to walk on the left side, but either side is fine. Just stick with one or the other. A small dog constantly going from side to side can trip you or get stepped on. Keep your reward treats on that side as well. Use them to encourage the puppy, maintain his attention, and reward him for keeping

Maltese

pace. Use verbal encouragements to get him moving if he slows down or stops. If he forges ahead, make him come back to your side to get a treat.

This method can be used to revise bad leash habits. If your dog lags or stops, make him catch up to you for the treat. It helps if you can dole them out on the go. If he pulls ahead or lunges, maintain your pace to force him back to your side to get the treat. Suddenly reversing directions and offering a treat is a helpful trick. He will soon learn that paying attention to your walking pace is worthwhile.

Tricks
Once your dog knows the basic commands, these can be revised into tricks.

Shake Hands
Shaking hands is a classic. When your dog is sitting, tell him "Shake hands" and then take his paw and reward him. After a few tries, he will anticipate your actions and begin raising his paw toward your hand. Immediately reward this with plenty of treats and praise. Once he has mastered this exercise, you can teach him to shake with the right or left paw—a trick guaranteed to impress your friends.

Wave
Wave can be taught as a follow-up to shaking hands. Tell your dog "Sit" and "Shake hands." As he lifts his paw, keep your hand a bit out of reach, and make him lift his paw higher. Don't take his paw; instead, tell him "Wave," and reward him with treat and praise. Once

SENIOR DOG TIP
Training the Older Dog
Motivation through praise and rewards becomes even more important when working with an older dog. Revising habits takes time. Don't make the mistake of thinking that your older Maltese has learned something after a couple of successful responses. If one approach doesn't work, experiment with a different training method. There is no single right way to train a dog.

he gets used to this trick, start skipping the *shake hands* command, and just tell him to sit and wave.

Play Dead

Once your dog knows *down,* you can teach him to play dead. Put him in the *down* position, and gently push him over onto his side. As he rolls over, say "Play dead" and reward him. Encourage him to stay in that position by using the *stay* command and a tummy rub.

Clicker Training

Clicker training is a simple way to create positive associations between a behavior and a reward. Start by clicking the clicker and immediately rewarding your dog as soon as he pays attention. He will soon learn that "click" means "reward." Once he makes this connection, you can use it to teach basic commands. For example, click at the same time you tell him to sit, and reward him. The clicker is also a great way to reinforce routine good behavior, something that's often overlooked during training.

Start training early and you'll have a well-behaved Maltese.

Chapter **7**

In the

Doghouse

A few dogs suffer from severe behavior anomalies, but most canine misbehavior can be traced to inept or inadequate training. A dog's ability to meet your training expectations depends on his temperament and training history. If your Maltese needs a bit of remedial training, take heart. Dogs are never too old to learn.

Some of the most common remedial training problems include barking, chewing, digging, house soiling, and jumping up.

Barking

Puppies usually start barking around three to four months of age. Some bloodlines are more prone to this habit, but every puppy has the potential. Dogs bark to get attention or relieve stress or boredom, and the behavior can easily evolve into a problem if it is ignored or rewarded. In many cases, puppies get into the habit of excessive barking thanks to human reinforcement. A little puppy barking at you to demand attention or a taste of your dinner may seem harmless. As soon as he realizes this strategy works (which won't take long), he will use it more and more. Voila! You have created a chronic barker.

Puppies are born knowing how to whine. They do it when they are cold, hungry, or simply want their mom—and it works like a charm.

Puppies continue to rely on the same tactics after making the transition to a human family. Plenty of things can prompt whining, but very few of them actually merit immediate attention. If it doesn't get the desired results, it will stop. But this behavior just as easily can be reinforced if humans sympathetically respond to it.

Many owners reward chronic barking and whining without even realizing it. If your dog barks to demand his dinner or walk, you may unconsciously hurry up to comply simply to quiet him down. Before long, you will find yourself caught in a vicious cycle of trying to stop more and more dog demands that trigger increasingly longer and louder barking.

Training, socialization, and proper exercise can help ward off many problem behaviors.

Whenever your Maltese commences unwanted barking, tell him to be quiet. Don't do anything until he obeys. And don't be worried that this may undermine his effectiveness as a watchdog. Training him to refrain from unwarranted barking will have the opposite effect. A watchdog who barks all the time is useless.

Teaching *Speak* and *Quiet*

This may seem like contradictory advice, but teaching your dog to bark is the best way to teach him to be quiet. Basically, you are installing an "on/off" switch.

Teaching your Maltese to speak on command can quiet down a chronic barker, because he will learn when to bark *and* when to stop. To teach this, do something that usually gets your dog barking, like rattling his dinner dish. When he starts, say "Speak" or "Bark," followed by praise. After a few seconds, tell him "Quiet," and show him the treat. He will be forced to stop barking to take his reward. Wait a couple of seconds after he stops barking before giving the treat, and add the command "Quiet" when that happens. Eventually, he will make the connection between "Speak" and barking, and you can phase out the dish rattling prompt.

Clicker training is a great reinforcer when teaching the *speak* and *quiet* commands. A basic obedience course can also help your dog to learn some self-control and redirect his obsessive tendencies. It can also benefit extremely sensitive dogs who bark at

FAMILY-FRIENDLY TIP

Safety First

Your child's safety should be your first consideration when managing a dog with behavior problems. Make sure that the child understands that the dog has a special problem. Describe exactly how to recognize it and what is likely to trigger or magnify it. Depending on the child's age and the nature of the problem, she may be able to participate in rehab therapy. It may be best to instruct the child to notify you immediately whenever she notices this behavior in the dog.

every little thing. This is often caused by a need for more socialization.

Chewing

Luckily, destructive chewing rarely becomes a chronic problem for Maltese. But your dog is going to chew on something, especially when he's teething. All dogs love to chew, so don't expect to train your dog to stop chewing. Chewing actually does have benefits: It's a great way to keep your dog occupied for long stretches of time, and it helps to keep his teeth in good condition.

Make sure that your dog has safe, healthy chew toys that appeal to him.

Otherwise, it will be impossible to redirect unwanted chewing from the chair leg to the toy. Knotted ropes, rawhides, tennis balls, and nylon bones rate high with most dogs. Many dogs love hard rubber toys designed to hold hidden treats.

Puppies need to chew, so provide your Maltese with plenty of appropriate chew toys.

Don't overwhelm him with too many toys at one time. This will make it harder for him to distinguish between what he is supposed to chew on and what is off-limits.

Supervision is the only way to prevent unwanted chewing. When you discover your Maltese chomping away on your new shoe, tell him "No," and redirect him to one of his toys. This doesn't guarantee that you won't find him sampling your new hat later on if you don't keep an eye on him. Chewing deterrents like bitter apple or oil of cloves sometimes help to create an aversion to chewing the table legs or kitchen cabinets. For some dogs, though, deterrents have the opposite effect.

Some dogs resort to chronic chewing to relieve boredom or stress. In these cases, you may need to reevaluate your dog's daily routine and make some changes. Every dog needs some regular daily exercise, even toy breeds like the Maltese. This can range from a rousing play session to a long, leisurely walk in the park. Whatever you decide, exercise has the same beneficial effect of alleviating boredom and expending excess energy. Inadequate exercise is one of the most common root causes of myriad canine bad habits.

Digging

Digging is a natural dog pastime. Some breeds, like Dachshunds, are more addicted to it than others, but any dog may turn to it to relieve boredom. Digging not only wrecks your garden, but it will wreak havoc with a Maltese coat. To prevent this behavior, you can provide your dog with a sandbox for cleaner, safer digging. Otherwise, you must do a better job of supervising him when he is outdoors, and provide satisfying outlets to relieve his boredom. Dogs should not be expected to spend hours a day trying to amuse themselves alone in the backyard.

House Soiling

Housetraining lapses can have mental, physical, or environmental causes. Good

observation is vital to discover the reason before it becomes a habit. It may be something simple like a diet change, or it could be a medical problem. If your vet rules out an underlying physical cause, you will need to do some detective work.

A common mistake is assuming that a housetrained dog doesn't need any remedial training when introduced to a new home. Whether you are bringing home a new dog or moving to a new home with your housetrained dog, it's your responsibility to tell him when and where he should eliminate. Otherwise,

Retraining

Retraining older dogs takes more effort because their bad habits are more ingrained. These habits must be stopped and replaced with new ones, and you will need consistency and patience to accomplish this. The most important thing to remember is that your dog isn't going to understand that he did something wrong until you establish a pattern of rewarding him for doing the right thing. This takes time and is sometimes frustrating. Keeping a training log provides a realistic picture of your progress.

he will inevitably devise his own rules about this.

All sorts of major or minor changes in a dog's environment or routine can cause housetraining lapses. Perhaps you have reseeded your lawn and decided that part of it is now off-limits to the dog. Or your neighbors have acquired a dog who intimidates your Maltese when he goes out to do his business. Bad weather can be enough of a reason for many small dogs. Changes in your daily schedule might also be the source of the problem. Have you been working late or failing to come home and walk the dog midday?

Adolescent leg lifting usually begins around five or six months of age. From a dog's point of view, the urge to go is just one of many good reasons to urinate. At this age, a normally housetrained dog can be tempted to break the rules for social, territorial, and sexual reasons. Curbing this habit requires reinforcing basic rules of housetraining through behavior modification, rewards, and good observation. For some dogs, training pants or bellybands are helpful to discourage territorial marking.

Constantly reprimanding your Maltese about housetraining issues can make existing problems worse. It may give him the idea that he's never supposed to eliminate any time or place when you are present and start sneaking off to do his business. Housetraining becomes a lot more complicated if a dog resorts to this strategy. The last thing you want to do is turn a housetraining problem into a major behavior modification project.

Most housetraining failures stem from the fact that many dogs aren't

In the Doghouse

adequately trained the first time around. This is usually traceable to one or more oversights, including:

- Was the dog carefully supervised, or did he have free run of the house before he was completely trained?
- Did you stick to his feeding and exercise schedule, or was it frequently revised?
- Did you remember to reward him every single time he eliminated in the right place?

If your answer to any of these questions is no, you will have to bite the bullet and start from scratch.

Jumping Up

Just like whining, puppies arrive preprogrammed to jump on you for attention. A little white fur ball hurtling through the air may seem cute, but it's not universally appreciated. And once the habit is rewarded, it's hard to stop. You may not even realize that you are reinforcing it.

For example, your dog naturally becomes excited when you arrive home, and his adrenaline level rises. If you respond in kind, he becomes more excited. Before you know it, he is wildly careening around the house, jumping and barking like crazy. At this point, he would not even hear you if you told him to stop. This is a typical scenario for toy dogs, and it makes it easy for them to incur injuries, like broken legs.

If your Maltese is a jumper, it's going

to take some work to get this behavior under control. First of all, stop responding to it. Tell him to sit, and reward that behavior instead. This helps to cultivate his focus and self-control. Always reward calmness and ignore wild jumping.

Reprimanding a dog for jumping may stop it temporarily. But he will probably start looking for another way to expend his excess energy. You need to make sure that he has an appropriate way to channel his energy and enthusiasm. It's also critical that no one encourage the jumping. This includes all family members, dog walkers, groomers, and anyone your dog sees regularly. If one person allows your dog to jump, he cannot be expected to understand that it's okay sometimes but not other times.

Phobias and Fears

Like us, dogs can develop irrational fears about things like car rides or loud noises.

Digging is a natural pastime for dogs.

Finding a Lost Dog

This can happen to any dog no matter how carefully you look after your Maltese. Have a game plan ready just in case. Microchips and tattoos are excellent means of permanent ID, but an ID tag bearing your phone number is the best way to ensure that someone will contact you if they find your dog.

Don't waste a minute to begin searching when you discover that your dog missing. Enlist as much help as you can. Have someone drive around the area where he was last seen. Other members of the search party should go out on foot. To save time, post "missing dog" flyers as you search. The flyers should contain a brief description of your dog, a clear recent picture, the exact time and place where he was last seen, at least one contact phone number, and the promise of a reward. Print them on brightly colored paper to make them more visible. Use a staple gun to attach layers of five or six flyers at each location in case someone decides to rip one down for your phone number.

There is always a possibility that someone will have second- or thirdhand information about your dog's whereabouts. Contact every animal shelter, veterinarian, dog groomer, pet shop, and rescue group you can think of. Ask local businesses to post your flyers. Letter carriers, gardeners, and local delivery people often notice stray dogs during their rounds. Make sure that they know how to find you if they spot your dog.

Don't limit your search to obvious places because small dogs can get into unusual hiding places. If you have another dog, bring him along on your search. This may help to lure a frightened dog out of hiding. Try leaving a piece of familiar-smelling clothing or bedding where he was last seen. Many dogs stay in the vicinity and will try to find their way home.

Your Maltese may turn up many miles (km) away if a Good Samaritan has picked him up. Don't assume the worst, and don't be tempted to give up the search after a few days. You can expand your search through classified advertising and by posting your story to a national lost dog website, or contact a professional pet detective to assist you.

Finding a Behaviorist

Canine behaviorists can have varying credentials or none at all. For instance, veterinary behaviorists hold a graduate degree in animal behavior. Behavioral consultants are not subject to professional regulation. They may or may not have any formal degree or hands-on experience.

Regardless of background and expertise, your priority is finding someone who can help your dog. A precise clinical description of your dog's problem is useless without practical advice on how to correct it. A particular training philosophy or method may work well for some breeds or specific problems but won't be suitable for everything.

Ask your breeder, vet, or local dog clubs to recommend behaviorists who have successfully worked with Maltese. Get references or check with your local Better Business Bureau for background information. Visit the Animal Behavior Society website (www.animalbehavior. org) for more tips on finding a qualified behaviorist.

Regardless of credentials or endorsements, if you have reservations about an individual's ability or training methods, go elsewhere. If she doesn't know what she is doing, she can easily make your dog's problem worse.

Symptoms can range from pacing, whining, or hiding to drooling or shaking. Conventional behavior modification methods using gradual, repeated exposures are the most common treatment. Severe phobias may benefit from drug therapy, and alternative treatments like Rescue Remedy also work in many cases.

Don't inadvertently reinforce your dog's fears when trying to comfort him. Dogs can misinterpret this as praise for fearful behavior.

A recent study measuring dogs' stress levels during thunderstorms revealed that owners' efforts to calm their pets had no effect. However, the comforting presence of another dog markedly improved a dog's recovery time.

Separation Anxiety

Separation anxiety is an umbrella term used to explain a range of bad habits, like barking, house soiling, and destructive chewing, that happen when dogs are left alone. Many cases respond to behavior modification for those specific problems. Elementary training procedures such as acclimating a puppy to spending time alone, crate training, and basic obedience prevents or discourages many potential cases of full-blown separation phobia.

Dogs are pack animals and not naturally suited to being alone, but most dogs manage to adjust to it. True separation anxiety causes a dog to experience extreme anxiety when left alone. He will often resort to typical canine stress relievers like barking and chewing, but it can also lead to physical symptoms like self-mutilation, diarrhea,

When to Seek Professional Help

Most canine misbehavior can be revised with dedicated training. However, some problems require professional evaluation and expert management from a trainer or behaviorist. Aggression toward humans or other pets definitely merits professional help. Not only does this behavior pose a danger (and potential lawsuits), but unless you know what you are doing, remedial training can worsen the problem. Dogs suffering from extreme anxiety or hyperactivity also may need professional help. A dog in this state will not respond to training. Behavior modification may need to be combined with medical therapy.

vomiting, or refusal to eat.

The problem can be due to a biochemical imbalance, inadequate puppy socialization, or severe trauma. Some cases can be treated with anti-anxiety medications or alternative therapies. Most are treated with behavior modification.

Make sure that you are not exacerbating your dog's fear of separation. For example, don't get him overly excited before you leave or when you return home. Keep your arrivals and departures as low-key as possible. Make sure that he is well exercised and tired before you leave. Confine him to an area where he cannot do damage to your home or himself, and provide plenty of interesting toys to amuse him in your absence.

Gradually accustom him to spending time separated from you when you are home. Crate him for short periods, or confine him to one room with a baby gate. This may be just a

couple of minutes. It should be long enough to familiarize him with isolation but not long enough to trigger an anxiety attack. Reward him (calmly) for positive responses like sitting quietly or playing with a toy.

If you feel that your dog's anxiety is getting out of control, don't hesitate to get help from a trainer or behaviorist whom you trust.

91

If you see a change in your Maltese's behavior, you may want to consult a professional.

Chapter 8

Stepping Out

You probably acquired your Maltese as a companion. No question, they excel in that role. But that's far from all they can do. These smart, energetic, athletic little dogs have many talents. You can participate in organized activities like agility or showing, or you can even take your petite pooch on vacation with you.

Organized Sports and Activities

There are many activities for you and your Maltese that can get your competitive juices flowing. To learn more, visit www.americanmaltese.org (American Maltese Association), www.akc.org (American Kennel Club), or www.ukcdogs.com (United Kennel Club).

Agility

Agility is possibly the most fun and exciting activity that you can do with your Maltese. Be warned, it's addictive! Small, agile, naturally athletic breeds like Maltese are physically suited to do very well at this sport. They love the mental and physical challenges posed by different exercises and varying obstacle courses.

The idea of competitive agility was based on the sport of horse show jumping. The basic routine includes 16 to 20 obstacles—a mixture of tunnels, chutes, hurdles, A-frames, and weave poles. Some courses are more complex, with things like bridges and contact obstacles that the dog must touch with his paw when running the course.

Agility training classes are offered through many kennel clubs and training classes. If your Maltese turns out to be a natural agility star, you may want to try entering competitive agility trials. Contact the American Kennel Club (AKC), United Kennel Club (UKC), United States Dog Agility Association (USDAA), or the North American Dog Agility Council (NADAC) to find upcoming trials in your area.

Be sure to familiarize yourself with the rules before entering. Competitions offer different levels of classes for beginners, experts, and dogs of different sizes. Many also provide classes for handlers less than 18 years of age, disabled handlers, and rescue dogs. Entrants receive a map of the obstacle course showing the route and obstacles that the dog must navigate. Most competitions also permit an advance "walk-through" to familiarize you with the course. Winners earn titles and become eligible to compete at the next level.

Obedience

Most Maltese complete a basic obedience class as part of their puppy training and socialization. If it turns out that you and your dog really enjoy this activity, you may want to try competitive obedience.

Most all-breed dog shows offer classes for novice and advanced obedience competitors. Beginning competitors must complete basic obedience exercises on lead. At more advanced levels, dogs must perform the exercises off lead,

Maltese

Agility Fact

The first Maltese to score 100 at an agility trial was Springtime Stanley J CDX, MX, AXJ, AAD, TDI, owned by Marilyn Jensen.

Agility is a fast-paced, exciting sport for dogs.

including retrieving, jumping, and locating articles by scent. Obedience competitors can earn titles ranging from Companion Dog (CD), requiring three qualifying scores in basic obedience competition, to Utility Dog Excellent (UDX), for dogs who have earned ten qualifying scores in advanced competition.

For information about obedience competitions in your area, contact the AKC or UKC.

Showing (Conformation)

If you want to show your Maltese in conformation, plan to devote time to training and grooming. There is a tremendous amount of work and skill involved in growing a coat to show length, properly maintaining it, and preparing it for exhibition. Ask an experienced Maltese exhibitor or professional handler for advice to get you started, and be prepared to practice, practice, practice.

Training your Maltese for conformation shows is a bit easier. Find a conformation training class through your local kennel club. This is the easiest way for you and your dog to learn the ropes together. You will need to know how to:

- "Stack": Pose your dog for examination on a table and on the floor.
- "Gait": Move your dog around the ring at the right speed to show his movement to the best advantage.
- "Bait": Encourage your dog to pose himself to catch the judge's eye.

Obedience Facts

- Last year, the AKC began offering three levels of awards in rally obedience, a faster paced and less formal obedience competition. It is quickly proving to be one of the most popular events at most dog shows.
- Since 1979, the American Maltese Association (AMA) has offered classes and awards for top scoring obedience dogs at their annual show. The first Maltese to be awarded High in Trial was Muff of Buckeye Circle, UD, owned by Ida Marsland.

The judge will evaluate your dog to determine the quality of his structure, temperament, and special breed traits, such as a flawless white coat and rich black pigment. Needless to say, your ability to groom and handle (present) your dog will have a great bearing on the judge's impression. Champion show dogs and professional handlers make this look effortless, which is a major part of the challenge. In reality, it takes many months or years of dedicated work.

After you've had some practice training your Maltese, enter him in a few "match" shows. These are small practice shows where no championship points are awarded. The entry fees are inexpensive, and it's a great way to gain confidence in an informal setting before taking the big step to "point" shows. Contact the AKC, UKC, or various dog show superintendents around the country to find upcoming point shows in your area. Entries must be made three weeks in advance.

Most point shows are "all-breed" classes are offered for all recognized purebreds. Non-champion Maltese of each sex compete against each other to earn points toward their championship. After earning 15 points, a dog becomes an official champion. He can continue competing in the Best of Breed class against other Maltese champions. Winners of this class go on to compete against all other toy Best of Breed winners in group competition. The best dog from each group then goes forward to the final, most intensive competition of the show. One

Maltese show dogs must "stack" (pose) on the examination table.

dog from as many as 3,000 to 4,000 will be chosen as the Best in Show winner, a tremendous achievement for any dog.

Other Activities

If competition doesn't appeal to you, here are some activities that might be fun for you and your Maltese.

Hiking

Most dogs love nothing more than to accompany their owner on a long walk. Try hiking with your Maltese at a local park, nature preserve, or in the woods. He'll love the chance to explore, and you will find yourself stopping to look at things you would

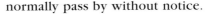

Conformation Facts

• The first Maltese AKC championship was awarded in 1901, to Thackery Rob Roy, and the breed's first Best In Show winner was Ch. Sweetsir of Dyiker, in 1912.

• The first Maltese to win a Westminster Toy Group was Ch. Co-Ca-He's Aennchen's Toy Dancer, in 1964, owned by Anna Marie Stimmler. She also won the first American Maltese Association Specialty show in 1966.

normally pass by without notice.

Check local regulations to make sure that dogs are permitted in your intended hiking territory. Apply tick repellent to both of you before starting out. Bring plenty of water, energy snacks, a first-aid kit, and cell phone. If there is potentially aggressive wildlife in the area, have a deterrent like pepper spray or lemon juice. A swan or a fox can easily tackle a Maltese.

Unless he is 100 percent reliable coming when called, keep your dog on lead, and always have him in sight at all times. A long flexi-lead can be perfect for this. Also, stop frequently to rest and drink. This will prevent the possibility of your dog deciding to drink from puddles or ponds. Bring along a dog carrier backpack, and pop him in for a ride if he gets

tired of hiking or if you get tired of keeping an eye on him. When you get home, comb through his coat to make sure that he has not picked up any ticks or burrs.

Swimming

Swimming is lots of fun, and it's one of the best overall forms of exercise for humans and dogs. In addition to lakes and beaches that permit dog swimming, many cities now have dog parks with special doggy beaches or pools.

Never take your dog swimming unless you are certain the water is safe and dogs are allowed. Monitor your dog constantly during swimming sessions. Don't hesitate to pull him out if he seems tired or disoriented. Even expert swimmers can go under if they become exhausted. Sunburn can also pose a risk for dogs. If there's a chance that you might sunburn, the same holds true for your Maltese.

athletic challenges. Don't forget to check his feet for soft pads, long nails, or weak tendons. Especially if he usually exercises on concrete or asphalt, check his foot pads regularly for sore spots or injuries. Obscured vision can lead to sports injuries, trim his bangs or keep his hair tied up in a topknot.

Comprehensive physical conditioning must include a range of activities to ensure that all muscles get a balanced workout. Try alternating activities designed to build strength, such as sprint running and endurance-building routines like swimming or jogging.

Your dog can't tell you if he is tired or sore, so it's your responsibility to make sure that he doesn't overdo it. Toys have less resistance to weather extremes, and exercise sessions should be limited or curtailed during very hot or cold weather. Your dog should only be exercised on lead or in a securely fenced area. Always keep an eye out for other potentially aggressive dogs; a small, fast-running dog can be seen as prey.

Wait at least two hours after your Maltese has eaten before allowing him to engage in strenuous exercise, and always have plenty of cool, fresh water available. Make sure that he stops to drink frequently rather than gulping down an entire bowl of water at once. Keep a high-energy treat available for him during workouts.

Always include a few minutes of warm-up and cool-down exercises before and after every session.

Sports safety requires that you evaluate your dog's physical ability and the potential hazards of his exercise environment.

Get your vet's okay before starting your Maltese on a formal exercise routine, especially if he is a bit out of condition. Overweight dogs should slim down to their ideal weight before commencing any rigorous sports, and growing puppies should limit participation to avoid overstressing growing bones and joints.

Every dog has some structural faults, but make sure that your dog is constructed well enough to tolerate sports activities. His front assembly carries more than half of his body weight, and it must be designed to cope with running and jumping. Ask your vet to make sure that his knee joints are sturdy. Loose patellas (kneecaps) might not cause a problem under normal circumstances, but they won't tolerate

Dry him thoroughly when he comes out of the water, because toys are more prone to chilling. And give him a bath when you get home to remove traces of salt water or chlorine that may irritate his skin or damage his coat.

Travel and Vacationing

One of the main advantages of owning a Maltese is that you can bring him just about anywhere with you. Not only are they portable, but they love to travel.

Your dog should have a complete vet exam prior to a major trip. If you are traveling by air, he will need vet

certification that he is healthy to fly. You may also need a copy of his vaccination records, depending on your destination. Bring a duplicate set in case the originals are lost in transit. Also, ask your vet if your dog will need extra flea or tick preventive when visiting certain climates. Spiders, bees, wasps, and lizards may also be a concern. Your vet can advise you on emergency treatment for insect and lizard bites.

Most airlines allow small dogs to travel in the cabin if they are in an approved carrier that will fit under the seat. If your Maltese will be traveling in an unfamiliar crate or carrier, introduce him to it at least a week before your trip. Sedating a dog for travel is not recommended, and many airlines do not accept sedated dogs for shipment.

Your Maltese will likely do most of his traveling by car. This is something that he should become accustomed to as a young puppy. Start with short trips, such as accompanying you on neighborhood errands. This also provides a good opportunity for puppy socialization. Never travel with your dog loose in the car, and never hold him on your lap while driving. Some owners prefer securing their dogs with a canine safety belt. For puppies and untrained dogs, a crate is usually a safer option. Make sure that it is securely placed and will not slide or bounce around while you are driving. If your Maltese exhibits signs of anxiety during the ride, cut it short and try again the

FAMILY-FRIENDLY TIP

On the Road

Traveling with your Maltese and your child requires good organizational skills. Start making a list of travel essentials well in advance of your trip, because there will be plenty. Designate a special travel bag for child essentials and dog essentials. Be flexible and open-minded, and don't let yourself stress out over minor details. Giving your child the responsibility of keeping the dog calm can serve a dual purpose of keeping both the child and dog occupied.

With just a few simple safety precautions, your Maltese can travel everywhere you go!

next day. Slow, positive acclimation is the best way to prevent travel sickness or car phobia.

Stick to your dog's normal routine as much as possible when traveling. A few items from home, like a favorite toy or blanket, may help him to settle into a new location. Small dogs are sometimes intolerant of unfamiliar tap water, so stick to bottled water.

Dogs are at greater risk of becoming lost in unfamiliar surroundings, which is why your Maltese should always wear a collar and ID tag when traveling. Always take him out on lead when visiting unfamiliar places, and always attach his lead before taking him out of a crate, car, or hotel room.

What to Pack

Your Maltese's most important travel accessory is a sturdy crate. When traveling with your dog in a small carrier bag, bring a more spacious folding crate with your baggage. Doggy essentials that you will need immediately on arrival should be packed in a carry-on bag. These include a leash, collar, water and water bowls, food, extra crate bedding, clean-up supplies and daily medications. If possible, bring a back-up supply of medication for your dog. This is much easier than trying

SENIOR DOG TIP

Traveling With Older Dogs

Maltese

Older dogs are less tolerant of change and more susceptible to stress, which can complicate traveling. Get your vet's okay before taking an older pet on a long trip. If your dog has a pre-existing health condition, be prepared to monitor him for potentially serious changes that may require immediate treatment.

Older dogs have a low tolerance for extremes of temperature. Use heating pads or crate fans to keep him comfortable during travel. Maintain his regular routine as much as possible. He may need more frequent walks to ensure that he doesn't have housetraining accidents. Also, make sure that he drinks enough water. If he is reluctant to drink, help him by squirting water into his mouth from a spray bottle.

to have his prescription refilled if it's lost when traveling.

Pack a basic first-aid kit, including phone numbers of vets and emergency clinics near your destination. If you are visiting a different climate, your dog may need appropriate weather gear or crate covers, heat disks, cold packs, or portable crate fans to keep him comfortable. Dogs tend to be more sensitive to heat or cold if they are not used to it. You'll also need bathing and grooming supplies, dog food and treats, and dishes.

For More Information

For more canine travel tips, visit these websites:

- American Dog Owners Association (www.adoa.com): for tips on traveling with dogs.
- American Kennel Club (www.akc. org/public_education/travel_tips. cfm): for ideas on how to safely travel with dogs.
- US Department of Agriculture (www.aphis.usda.gov/vs/ncie/iregs/ animals): for international animal export regulations.
- US Department of Transportation (www. Airconsumer.ost.dot.gov/ reports): for animal handling safety records of various airlines.

Resources

Associations and Organizations

Breed Clubs

American Kennel Club (AKC)
5580 Centerview Drive
Raleigh, NC 27606
Telephone: (919) 233-9767
Fax: (919) 233-3627
E-mail: info@akc.org
www.akc.org

Canadian Kennel Club (CKC)
89 Skyway Avenue, Suite 100
Etobicoke, Ontario M9W 6R4
Telephone: (416) 675-5511
Fax: (416) 675-6506
E-mail: information@ckc.ca
www.ckc.ca

Federation Cynologique Internationale (FCI)
Secretariat General de la FCI
Place Albert 1er, 13
B – 6530 Thuin
Belqique
www.fci.be

The Kennel Club
1 Clarges Street
London
W1J 8AB
Telephone: 0870 606 6750
Fax: 0207 518 1058
www.the-kennel-club.org.uk

United Kennel Club (UKC)
100 E. Kilgore Road
Kalamazoo, MI 49002-5584
Telephone: (269) 343-9020
Fax: (269) 343-7037
E-mail: pbickell@ukcdogs.com
www.ukcdogs.com

Pet Sitters

National Association of Professional Pet Sitters
15000 Commerce Parkway, Suite C
Mt. Laurel, New Jersey 08054
Telephone: (856) 439-0324
Fax: (856) 439-0525
E-mail: napps@ahint.com
www.petsitters.org

Pet Sitters International
201 East King Street
King, NC 27021-9161
Telephone: (336) 983-9222
Fax: (336) 983-5266
E-mail: info@petsit.com
www.petsit.com

Rescue Organizations and Animal Welfare Groups

American Humane Association (AHA)
63 Inverness Drive East
Englewood, CO 80112
Telephone: (303) 792-9900
Fax: 792-5333
www.americanhumane.org

American Society for the Prevention of Cruelty to Animals (ASPCA)
424 E. 92nd Street
New York, NY 10128-6804
Telephone: (212) 876-7700
www.aspca.org

Royal Society for the Prevention of Cruelty to Animals (RSPCA)
Telephone: 0870 3335 999
Fax: 0870 7530 284
www.rspca.org.uk

Maltese

The Humane Society of the United States (HSUS)
2100 L Street, NW
Washington DC 20037
Telephone: (202) 452-1100
www.hsus.org

Sports
International Agility Link (IAL)
Global Administrator: Steve Drinkwater
E-mail: yunde@powerup.au
www.agilityclick.com/~ial

North American Dog Agility Council
11522 South Hwy 3
Cataldo, ID 83810
www.nadac.com

United States Dog Agility Association
P.O. Box 850955
Richardson, TX 75085-0955
Telephone: (972) 487-2200
www.usdaa.com

Therapy
Delta Society
875 124th Ave NE, Suite 101
Bellevue, WA 98005
Telephone: (425) 226-7357
Fax: (425) 235-1076
E-mail: info@deltasociety.org
www.deltasociety.org

Therapy Dogs Incorporated
PO Box 5868
Cheyenne, WY 82003
Telephone: (877) 843-7364
E-mail: therdog@sisna.com
www.therapydogs.com

Therapy Dogs International (TDI)
88 Bartley Road
Flanders, NJ 07836
Telephone: (973) 252-9800
Fax: (973) 252-7171
E-mail: tdi@gti.net
www.tdi-dog.org

Training
Association of Pet Dog Trainers (APDT)
150 Executive Center Drive Box 35
Greenville, SC 29615
Telephone: (800) PET-DOGS
Fax: (864) 331-0767
E-mail: information@apdt.com
www.apdt.com

National Association of Dog Obedience Instructors
PMB 369
729 Grapevine Hwy.
Hurst, TX 76054-2085
www.nadoi.org

Veterinary and Health Resources
Academy of Veterinary Homeopathy (AVH)
P.O. Box 9280
Wilmington, DE 19809
Telephone: (866) 652-1590
Fax: (866) 652-1590
E-mail: office@TheAVH.org
www.theavh.org

American Academy of Veterinary Acupuncture (AAVA)
100 Roscommon Drive, Suite 320
Middletown, CT 06457
Telephone: (860) 635-6300
Fax: (860) 635-6400
E-mail: office@aava.org
www.aava.org

American Animal Hospital Association (AAHA)
P.O. Box 150899
Denver, CO 80215-0899
Telephone: (303) 986-2800
Fax: (303) 986-1700
E-mail: info@aahanet.org
www.aahanet.org/index.cfm

American College of Veterinary Internal Medicine (ACVIM)
1997 Wadsworth Blvd., Suite A
Lakewood, CO 80214-5293
Telephone: (800) 245-9081
Fax: (303) 231-0880
Email: ACVIM@ACVIM.org
www.acvim.org

American College of Veterinary Ophthalmologists (ACVO)
P.O. Box 1311
Meridian, Idaho 83860
Telephone: (208) 466-7624
Fax: (208) 466-7693
E-mail: office@acvo.com
www.acvo.com

American Holistic Veterinary Medical Association (AHVMA)
2218 Old Emmorton Road
Bel Air, MD 21015
Telephone: (410) 569-0795
Fax: (410) 569-2346
E-mail: office@ahvma.org
www.ahvma.org

American Veterinary Medical Association (AVMA)
1931 North Meacham Road – Suite 100
Schaumburg, IL 60173
Telephone: (847) 925-8070
Fax: (847) 925-1329
E-mail: avmainfo@avma.org
www.avma.org

ASPCA Animal Poison Control Center
1717 South Philo Road, Suite 36
Urbana, IL 61802
Telephone: (888) 426-4435
www.aspca.org

British Veterinary Association (BVA)
7 Mansfield Street
London
W1G 9NQ
Telephone: 020 7636 6541
Fax: 020 7436 2970
E-mail: bvahq@bva.co.uk
www.bva.co.uk

Canine Eye Registration Foundation (CERF)
VMDB/CERF
1248 Lynn Hall
625 Harrison St.
Purdue University
West Lafayette, IN 47907-2026
Telephone: (765) 494-8179
E-mail: CERF@vmbd.org
www.vmdb.org

Orthopedic Foundation for Animals (OFA)
2300 NE Nifong Blvd
Columbus, Missouri 65201-3856
Telephone: (573) 442-0418
Fax: (573) 875-5073
E-mail: ofa@offa.org
www.offa.org

Publications

Books

Anderson, Teoti, *The Super Simple Guide to Housetraining*, Neptune, NJ: TFH Publications, 2004.

Morgan, Diane, *Good Dogkeeping*, Neptune, NJ: TFH Publications, 2005.

Silvani, Pia and Lynn Eckhardt, *Raising*

Maltese

Puppies and Kids Together: A Guide for Parents, Neptune, NJ: TFH Publications, 2005.

Yin, Sophia, DVM, *How to Behave So Your Dog Behaves*, Neptune, NJ: TFH Publications, 2004.

Magazines

AKC *Family Dog*
American Kennel Club
260 Madison Avenue
New York, NY 10016
Telephone: (800) 490-5675
E-mail: familydog@akc.org
www.akc.org/pubs/familydog

AKC *Gazette*
American Kennel Club
260 Madison Avenue
New York, NY 10016
Telephone: (800) 533-7323
E-mail: gazette@akc.org
www.akc.org/pubs/gazette

Dog & Kennel
Pet Publishing, Inc.
7-L Dundas Circle
Greensboro, NC 27407
Telephone: (336) 292-4272
Fax: (336) 292-4272
E-mail: info@petpublishing.com
www.dogandkennel.com

Dog Fancy
Subscription Department
P.O. Box 53264
Boulder, CO 80322-3264
Telephone: (800) 365-4421
E-mail: barkback@dogfancy.com
www.dogfancy.com

Dogs Monthly
Ascot House
High Street, Ascot,
Berkshire SL5 7JG
United Kingdom
Telephone: 0870 730 8433
Fax: 0870 730 8431
E-mail: admin@rtc-associates.freeserve.co.uk
www.corsini.co.uk/dogsmonthly

Index

Maltese

Note: Boldfaced numbers indicate illustrations.

111

Index

Acknowledgements

I would like to thank the breeders that contributed their expertise to the project, Glenna and Vicki Fierheller (Four Halls Maltese) and Barbara Bergquist (Su-Le Maltese).

About the Author

Freelance artist and writer Amy Fernandez has bred Chinese Cresteds since 1980. She has authored several books, including *Dog Breeding As A Fine Art*, winner of the prestigious DWAA Presidential Award of Excellence. She writes a monthly column for *Top Notch Toys* and writes for *Dog World*, *Popular Dogs*, the AKC *Gazette*, AKC *Family Dog* and *Dogs in Review*. Her *Dogs in Review* historical series won the 2004 and 2005 Elsworth Howell Award. She is vice president of the Dog Writers Association of America, president of the Xoloitzcuintli Club of America and editor of the "Xolo News." Her artwork can be viewed at www.amyfernandez.com.

Photo Credits

Josh Rodriguez (Shutterstock): 4
Leah-Anne Thompson (Shutterstock): 6
Chris Bence (Shutterstock): 32, 36 (left)
April Turner (Shutterstock): 34
Kenneth William Caleno (Shutterstock): 37 (top)
Robert Pearcy: 60, 101
Rayna Canedy (Dreamstime): 65, 103
Joy Brown (Shutterstock): 82
Theresa Martinez (Shutterstock): 98
Karen Roach (Dreamstime): 107
All other photos courtesy Isabelle Francais

Cover photo: Kenneth William Caleno (Shutterstock)